Unless otherwise indicated, all scripture quotations are from the King James Version of the Bible.

Published by:

Aggressive Faith Publishing Company

Plot 13 Walter Akpana Lay Out

Off 394 Ikwerre Road Mile 5 Rumueprikom

P. O. Box 12378,

Port Harcourt, Nigeria.

E-mail: info@aggressivefaith.org

Web site: www.aggressivefaith.org

Phone: +2349018006296, +2348050987377

+2348036732188 (WhatsApp/Text/Voice)

+1-916-245-6157 (U.S.A.)

ISBN: 978-978-51071-7-3

Printed in the Federal Republic of Nigeria

Dedication

I dedicate this devotional to the amazing medical professionals who have been on the frontlines helping people recover from the corona virus pandemic.

I also dedicate it to everyone who survived the lockdown for several months.

It was tough but we survived.

Introduction

Vernon Law said, *'Experience is a hard teacher because she gives the test first, the lesson afterward.'* Most valuable lessons of life are learnt when we experience them.

I am very certain that David knew a bit about God before Saul started hunting for his life. Think about it, if the President of the United States of America wants you dead, how can you escape? King Saul wanted David dead. All David had was God and God gave him victory.

"I will love thee, O Lord, my strength.

The Lord is my rock, and my fortress, and my deliverer; my God, my strength, in whom I will trust; my buckler, and the horn of my salvation, and my high tower."

David shows us nine things he discovered about God that helped him through his flight from Saul. These nine discoveries about God can change your life in times of fright or flight or fight like these.

1. The Lord is my rock. Two things about rocks are that they are large and solid. They can hold you just as much as you can hold them. The Lord is large and solid. You can hold Him just as much as He can hold you. Any life or marriage or family or business or ministry that is built on the rock can survive any wind or wave.

2. The Lord is my fortress. A fortress is a military stronghold. It is a defense headquarters. The Lord is your defense headquarters that no enemy can penetrate.

3. The Lord is my deliverer. He is the One who can cause your escape. How else could David have escaped every assault and attack from Saul? The Lord delivered him. The Lord can deliver you from anything, anyone or any place.

4. The Lord is my God. A god is anything or anyone you run to for help because you consider them superior or supreme or superhuman. Who is your god? When the Lord is your God, He becomes supreme and superior to all others in your life.

5. The Lord is my strength. Your strength is usually the one who has power to help you. When you have a problem or battle, who is your strength? Who do you rely on to help you prevail? That is your strength.

6. The Lord is my buckler. A buckler is a shield that wards off arrows and darts. People will shoot arrows and darts at you. The big question is: who is your buckler? Who knocks off those darts and arrows for you?

7. The Lord is the horn of my salvation. The horn of salvation is the power to save and make safe. In times like these when your life is endangered, who is the horn of your salvation? Who guaranties you are saved and safe? Is it God or government?

8. The Lord is my high tower. A high tower is an inaccessible place and a vantage position due to altitude. When the Lord is your high tower, you can become impervious and inaccessible to your enemies.

9. The Lord is my trust. What gives you that strong confidence and assurance that no matter what happens to the economy or government, you are secured? Only the Lord can give this kind of assurance.

Every day for the next thirty days, can you exercise yourself by declaring these nine things about God to yourself? I will do it because like David, I have seen God in all these nine ways in my short life on earth. I believe and declare from today, ***The Lord is….***

DAY ONE

Welcome to the beginning of your confession of faith!

Today we begin our daily confessions of God's word for the next 30 days.

"And say thou unto the people, Sanctify yourselves against to morrow, and ye shall eat flesh: for ye have wept in the ears of the Lord, saying, Who shall give us flesh to eat? for it was well with us in Egypt: therefore the Lord will give you flesh, and ye shall eat.

Ye shall not eat one day, nor two days, nor five days, neither ten days, nor twenty days;

But even a whole month, until it come out at your nostrils, and it be loathsome unto you: because that ye have despised the Lord which is among you, and have wept before him, saying, Why came we forth out of Egypt?

And Moses said, The people, among whom I am, are six hundred thousand footmen; and thou hast said, I will give them flesh, that they may eat a whole month.

Shall the flocks and the herds be slain for them, to suffice them? or shall all the fish of the sea be gathered together for them, to suffice them?

And the Lord said unto Moses, Is the Lord's hand waxed short? thou shalt see now whether my word shall come to pass unto thee or not."

Num. 11:18-23.

Before I lead you on this journey if you will, let me share with you a word from Numbers 11:18-23. The people complained and murmured about what to eat in times like this.

God heard their murmurings. So God hears murmurings too.

In response, God said to them, **I will give you what to eat for a whole month.**

God will give you what to eat this month. You will not need to steal or die because of the lockdown.

In verse 23, God asked Moses, Is My hand waxed short? Have I lost My ability to provide? You will SEE that My word works.

Since God's provision is linked with your confession, I encourage you to make this confession every day for the rest of the month. As God said, you will SEE that His word works.

CONFESSION FOR THE MONTH

I believe and declare,

The Lord is my Rock. He is large and solid for me. He can hold me just as I can hold Him. I choose to hold on to Him and His word in the name of Jesus Christ my Lord.

The Lord is my Fortress. He is my stronghold and defense headquarters. As long as I am in Him, no plague can penetrate me. I am safe in Him.

The Lord is my Deliverer. He causes me to escape every assault and attack from the enemy. I am delivered from the plague in the name of Jesus Christ my Lord.

The Lord is my God. I have no other God but Jehovah God. Jehovah Jireh is my God. The El Shaddai is my God. The government is not my God. My God is Supreme and Superior to all. His judgment nullifies all others.

The Lord is my Strength. He empowers, energizes and emboldens me to overcome all tests, trials, troubles, tribulations and temptations. I totally depend on the Lord who strengthens me to overcome this month in the name of Jesus Christ my Lord.

The Lord is my Buckler. He shields me from every dart, arrow and plague shot at me. He wards them off from me. That is why no plague touches me. No sickness or disease or infection or virus touches me. I am safe in Christ Jesus my Lord.

The Lord is the Horn of my Salvation. He saves me and keeps me safe. I am saved and safe in Christ Jesus my Lord.

The Lord is my High Tower. I am impervious and inaccessible to all plagues and pestilence. No evil shall befall me. No plague shall come near me. I have a vantage position. I am not disadvantaged. I have the advantage because the Lord is my High Tower.

The Lord is my Trust. I am secured, insured and assured because I trust in the Lord Jesus Christ. I am not moved by the government or economy or news. I am moved by God's word that guarantees my security and supplies in the name of Jesus Christ my Lord. Amen.

As you make these confessions, watch out for what God is doing. He said that you will SEE His word works. See only His word. Nothing else.

DAY TWO

Welcome to the second day of our confession of faith!

As we continue making our confessions for the month, I want to remind you of what God said in Numbers 11:18-23. God promised to give you food the whole of this month.

Thank God that He is not the government. The government is not God. If you keep your ears glued to what some of these government officials are saying, you may be heading to an early grave.

"For unto us a child is born, unto us a son is given: and the government shall be upon his shoulder: and his name shall be called Wonderful, Counsellor, The mighty God, The everlasting Father, The Prince of Peace.

Of the increase of his government and peace there shall be no end, upon the throne of David, and upon his kingdom, to order it, and to establish it with judgment and with justice from henceforth even for ever. The zeal of the Lord of hosts will perform this."

Isa. 9:6-7.

The government is upon His shoulder and one characteristic feature of His government is peace not the confusion we are seeing around us.

Take your eyes and ears away from the news media and focus them on God this month. If you look at the government, you will complain until you die. You can imagine all the fifty million Euros donated to the Nigerian government by the European Union besides other donations in billions of naira, yet the government palliative to a few people was five thousand naira or a pack of noodles or half tuber of yam for a family. That can't feed a baby for one day. Is that the government you want to look up to? Your provision and protection will come from God not the government.

Make these confessions because your provision and supplies in this season are tied to your confession. You will SEE what you SAY. SAY what you want to SEE.

CONFESSION FOR THE MONTH

I believe and declare,

The Lord is my Rock. He is large and solid for me. He can hold me just as I can hold Him. I choose to hold on to Him and His word in the name of Jesus Christ my Lord.

The Lord is my Fortress. He is my stronghold and defense headquarters. As long as I am in Him, no plague can penetrate me. I am safe in Him.

The Lord is my Deliverer. He causes me to escape every assault and attack from the enemy. I am delivered from the plague in the name of Jesus Christ my Lord.

The Lord is my God. I have no other God but Jehovah God. Jehovah Jireh is my God. The El Shaddai is my God. The government is not my God. My God is Supreme and Superior to all. His judgment nullifies all others.

The Lord is my Strength. He empowers, energizes and emboldens me to overcome all tests, trials, troubles, tribulations and temptations. I totally depend on the Lord who strengthens me to overcome this month in the name of Jesus Christ my Lord.

The Lord is my Buckler. He shields me from every dart, arrow and plague shot at me. He wards them off from me. That is why no plague touches me. No sickness or disease or infection or virus touches me. I am safe in Christ Jesus my Lord.

The Lord is the Horn of my Salvation. He saves me and keeps me safe. I am saved and safe in Christ Jesus my Lord.

The Lord is my High Tower. I am impervious and inaccessible to all plagues and pestilence. No evil shall befall me. No plague shall come near me. I have a vantage position. I am not disadvantaged. I have the advantage because the Lord is my High Tower.

The Lord is my Trust. I am secured, insured and assured because I trust in the Lord Jesus Christ. I am not moved by the government or economy or news. I am moved by God's word that guarantees my security and supplies in the name of Jesus Christ my Lord. Amen.

As you make these confessions, watch out for what God is doing. He said that you will SEE His word works. See only His word. Nothing else.

DAY THREE

Welcome to the third day of our confession of faith!

As we continue making our confessions for the next 30 days, I want to remind you of what God said in Numbers 11:18-23. God promised to give you food the whole of this month.

Like Moses, sometimes, we ask God, do You know what You are talking about? Are You going to do exactly what You said? Moses wanted God to know that he counted 600,000 soldiers besides those under aged, women and children. To further help God, Moses asked God even if He killed all the fishes in the river and animals, would they be enough for the people? You know how insatiable human needs are.

I can understand Moses because I have been there many times and even now. I know what it feels like when God tells you He will feed you and you don't see how.

However, when you have experienced God's miraculous provision once or twice or more, you become confident that no matter how impossible it looks like now, God will definitely make His word work.

Can you remember one instance when God provided even when you never knew how He would be able to? Think about that for a few minutes.

One brother testified when we made these confessions through the month of April 2020. He joined us the second week while his entire family joined the third week. He said, *I can humbly say April was the best month so far. We never lacked, none was sick or weak and we had so much joy and peace…we even shared some of our surplus with those in need around us and far…* Pastor Kingrichard Joe.

Make your confessions because you know God will not fail just like He didn't that time and now for Pastor Joe.

CONFESSION FOR THE MONTH

I believe and declare,

The Lord is my Rock. He is large and solid for me. He can hold me just as I can hold Him. I choose to hold on to Him and His word in the name of Jesus Christ my Lord.

The Lord is my Fortress. He is my stronghold and defense headquarters. As long as I am in Him, no plague can penetrate me. I am safe in Him.

The Lord is my Deliverer. He causes me to escape every assault and attack from the enemy. I am delivered from the plague in the name of Jesus Christ my Lord.

The Lord is my God. I have no other God but Jehovah God. Jehovah Jireh is my God. The El Shaddai is my God. The government is not my God. My God is Supreme and Superior to all. His judgment nullifies all others.

The Lord is my Strength. He empowers, energizes and emboldens me to overcome all tests, trials, troubles, tribulations and temptations. I totally depend on the Lord who strengthens me to overcome this month in the name of Jesus Christ my Lord.

The Lord is my Buckler. He shields me from every dart, arrow and plague shot at me. He wards them off from me. That is why no plague touches me. No sickness or disease or infection or virus touches me. I am safe in Christ Jesus my Lord.

The Lord is the Horn of my Salvation. He saves me and keeps me safe. I am saved and safe in Christ Jesus my Lord.

The Lord is my High Tower. I am impervious and inaccessible to all plagues and pestilence. No evil shall befall me. No plague shall come near me. I have a vantage position. I am not disadvantaged. I have the advantage because the Lord is my High Tower.

The Lord is my Trust. I am secured, insured and assured because I trust in the Lord Jesus Christ. I am not moved by the government or economy or news. I am moved by God's word that guarantees my security and supplies in the name of Jesus Christ my Lord. Amen.

As you make these confessions, watch out for what God is doing. He said that you will SEE His word works. See only His word. Nothing else.

DAY FOUR

Welcome to the fourth day of our confession of faith!

As we continue making our confessions for the next 30 days, I want to remind you of what God said in Numbers 11:18-23. God promised to give you food the whole of this month.

You probably have heard the saying that only Nigerians use question to answer question. I noticed that God does that too. May be Nigerians are closer to God than any other people.

In answer to Moses question, God asked Moses, Do you think I can't take care of you? Numbers 11:23. However, God is so different from us that when He asks you a question, He doesn't wait for your answer. He goes on to answer His own question in answer to your question.

What questions have you been asking God? Today, God has answered your questions. He said, you will SEE whether His word will happen to you or not. SEE His word working. SEE His word works.

Make your confessions today because you SEE His word works for you.

CONFESSION FOR THE MONTH

I believe and declare,

The Lord is my Rock. He is large and solid for me. He can hold me just as I can hold Him. I choose to hold on to Him and His word in the name of Jesus Christ my Lord.

The Lord is my Fortress. He is my stronghold and defense headquarters. As long as I am in Him, no plague can penetrate me. I am safe in Him.

The Lord is my Deliverer. He causes me to escape every assault and attack from the enemy. I am delivered from the plague in the name of Jesus Christ my Lord.

The Lord is my God. I have no other God but Jehovah God. Jehovah Jireh is my God. The El Shaddai is my God. The government is not my God. My God is Supreme and Superior to all. His judgment nullifies all others.

The Lord is my Strength. He empowers, energizes and emboldens me to overcome all tests, trials, troubles, tribulations and temptations. I totally depend on the Lord who strengthens me to overcome this month in the name of Jesus Christ my Lord.

The Lord is my Buckler. He shields me from every dart, arrow and plague shot at me. He wards them off from me. That is why no plague touches me. No sickness or disease or infection or virus touches me. I am safe in Christ Jesus my Lord.

The Lord is the Horn of my Salvation. He saves me and keeps me safe. I am saved and safe in Christ Jesus my Lord.

The Lord is my High Tower. I am impervious and inaccessible to all plagues and pestilence. No evil shall befall me. No plague shall come near me. I have a vantage position. I am not disadvantaged. I have the advantage because the Lord is my High Tower.

The Lord is my Trust. I am secured, insured and assured because I trust in the Lord Jesus Christ. I am not moved by the government or economy or news. I am moved by God's word that guarantees my security and supplies in the name of Jesus Christ my Lord. Amen.

As you make these confessions, watch out for what God is doing. He said that you will SEE His word works. See only His word. Nothing else.

DAY FIVE

Welcome to the fifth day of our confession of faith!

For the first time in all my short life on earth a tiny virus changed the way we celebrate Palm Sunday and the week commemorating the suffering, death, burial and resurrection of our Lord Jesus Christ. If this attack is not an assault against Christ, what else?

You can see the power of confession in the life of our Lord Jesus Christ. In Matt. 27:63, His killers repeated what they heard Him say several times. He said it several times, *After three days, I will rise again*. No matter how down you are right now, believe and declare, **I will rise again.**

Look at your food storage, fuel tank and finances and declare to them, **I will rise again!**

As we continue making our confessions for the rest of the month, I want to remind you of what God said in Numbers 11:18-23. God promised to give you food the whole of this month. Do you believe God? I believe!

CONFESSION FOR THE MONTH

I believe and declare,

The Lord is my Rock. He is large and solid for me. He can hold me just as I can hold Him. I choose to hold on to Him and His word in the name of Jesus Christ my Lord.

The Lord is my Fortress. He is my stronghold and defense headquarters. As long as I am in Him, no plague can penetrate me. I am safe in Him.

The Lord is my Deliverer. He causes me to escape every assault and attack from the enemy. I am delivered from the plague in the name of Jesus Christ my Lord.

The Lord is my God. I have no other God but Jehovah God. Jehovah Jireh is my God. The El Shaddai is my God. The government is not my God. My God is Supreme and Superior to all. His judgment nullifies all others.

The Lord is my Strength. He empowers, energizes and emboldens me to overcome all tests, trials, troubles, tribulations and temptations. I totally depend on the Lord who strengthens me to overcome this month in the name of Jesus Christ my Lord.

The Lord is my Buckler. He shields me from every dart, arrow and plague shot at me. He wards them off from me. That is why no plague touches me. No sickness or disease or infection or virus touches me. I am safe in Christ Jesus my Lord.

The Lord is the Horn of my Salvation. He saves me and keeps me safe. I am saved and safe in Christ Jesus my Lord.

The Lord is my High Tower. I am impervious and inaccessible to all plagues and pestilence. No evil shall befall me. No plague shall come near me. I have a vantage position. I am not disadvantaged. I have the advantage because the Lord is my High Tower.

The Lord is my Trust. I am secured, insured and assured because I trust in the Lord Jesus Christ. I am not moved by the government or economy or news. I am moved by God's word that guarantees my security and supplies in the name of Jesus Christ my Lord. Amen.

As you make these confessions, watch out for what God is doing. He said that you will SEE His word works. See only His word. Nothing else.

DAY SIX

Welcome to the sixth day of our confession of faith!

Remember, God created man on the sixth day. Gen. 1:31. How man was created shows us how man can be sustained. How was man created? Gen. 1:26, ***And God said, Let us make man in our image, after our likeness...***

First, you see that man was created by the spoken word. ***And God said.*** Man is the result of confession or proclamation or prophesy or preaching. You are the product of words.

Second, God made man after His image. God's image is His word when spoken. Man looks like God when He speaks like God. Your daily confession is making you look exactly like what you confess. If what you are today are the results of your confessions yesterday, what would you like to look like tomorrow? Can you start today to become more responsible, resolute and radical about your confessions about what your tomorrow should be?

As we continue making our confessions for the rest of the month, I want to remind you of what God said in Numbers 11:18-23. God promised to give you food the whole of this month.

CONFESSION FOR THE MONTH

I believe and declare,

The Lord is my Rock. He is large and solid for me. He can hold me just as I can hold Him. I choose to hold on to Him and His word in the name of Jesus Christ my Lord.

The Lord is my Fortress. He is my stronghold and defense headquarters. As long as I am in Him, no plague can penetrate me. I am safe in Him.

The Lord is my Deliverer. He causes me to escape every assault and attack from the enemy. I am delivered from the plague in the name of Jesus Christ my Lord.

The Lord is my God. I have no other God but Jehovah God. Jehovah Jireh is my God. The El Shaddai is my God. The government is not my God. My God is Supreme and Superior to all. His judgment nullifies all others.

The Lord is my Strength. He empowers, energizes and emboldens me to overcome all tests, trials, troubles, tribulations and temptations. I totally depend on the Lord who strengthens me to overcome this month in the name of Jesus Christ my Lord.

The Lord is my Buckler. He shields me from every dart, arrow and plague shot at me. He wards them off from me. That is why no plague touches me. No sickness or disease or infection or virus touches me. I am safe in Christ Jesus my Lord.

The Lord is the Horn of my Salvation. He saves me and keeps me safe. I am saved and safe in Christ Jesus my Lord.

The Lord is my High Tower. I am impervious and inaccessible to all plagues and pestilence. No evil shall befall me. No plague shall come near me. I have a vantage position. I am not disadvantaged. I have the advantage because the Lord is my High Tower.

The Lord is my Trust. I am secured, insured and assured because I trust in the Lord Jesus Christ. I am not moved by the government or economy or news. I am moved by God's word that guarantees my security and supplies in the name of Jesus Christ my Lord. Amen.

As you make these confessions, watch out for what God is doing. He said that you will SEE His word works. See only His word. Nothing else.

DAY SEVEN

Welcome to the seventh day of our confession of faith!

"And God said, Let us make man in our image, after our likeness…"

In Gen. 1:26, we see that man was created by God to look like God. Man can only look like God by looking at God. Man becomes a reflection of God on earth as he looks at God daily.

This is how you and I were designed to function. You didn't create yourself so you can't change yourself no matter how hard you try. You can only change by beholding your Creator. 2 Cor. 3:18 puts it this way, as we behold the glass of God's word, He changes us into His own image and that from glory to glory by His Spirit.

"But we all, with open face beholding as in a glass the glory of the Lord, are changed into the same image from glory to glory, even as by the Spirit of the Lord."

2 Cor. 3:18.

This is one truth that freed me back in the 80s when I was struggling to live the Christian life. One day, I cried to God that I don't think I can go far in this Christian life with all my weakness and failure. Then, God spoke to me, if your television has problem, what do you do? Does it fix itself? I said, no. I send it to the manufacturer. Only the manufacturer can fix it. He said, I am your manufacturer. I am the only One who can fix you. I can fix you if you allow My word into your life on a daily basis.

From that day, I developed the habit of reading, studying, meditating, memorizing, confessing and obeying God's word. I still fail today but I really don't bother because every day I allow His word to wash me.

Let's do some washing as we make our confessions today. It's time for my spiritual bath.

As we continue making our confessions for the rest of the month, I want to remind you of what God said in Numbers 11:18-23. God promised to give you food the whole of this month.

CONFESSION FOR THE MONTH

I believe and declare,

The Lord is my Rock. He is large and solid for me. He can hold me just as I can hold Him. I choose to hold on to Him and His word in the name of Jesus Christ my Lord.

The Lord is my Fortress. He is my stronghold and defense headquarters. As long as I am in Him, no plague can penetrate me. I am safe in Him.

The Lord is my Deliverer. He causes me to escape every assault and attack from the enemy. I am delivered from the plague in the name of Jesus Christ my Lord.

The Lord is my God. I have no other God but Jehovah God. Jehovah Jireh is my God. The El Shaddai is my God. The government is not my God. My God is Supreme and Superior to all. His judgment nullifies all others.

The Lord is my Strength. He empowers, energizes and emboldens me to overcome all tests, trials, troubles, tribulations and temptations. I totally depend on the Lord who strengthens me to overcome this month in the name of Jesus Christ my Lord.

The Lord is my Buckler. He shields me from every dart, arrow and plague shot at me. He wards them off from me. That is why no plague touches me. No sickness or disease or infection or virus touches me. I am safe in Christ Jesus my Lord.

The Lord is the Horn of my Salvation. He saves me and keeps me safe. I am saved and safe in Christ Jesus my Lord.

The Lord is my High Tower. I am impervious and inaccessible to all plagues and pestilence. No evil shall befall me. No plague shall come near me. I have a vantage position. I am not disadvantaged. I have the advantage because the Lord is my High Tower.

The Lord is my Trust. I am secured, insured and assured because I trust in the Lord Jesus Christ. I am not moved by the government or economy or news. I am moved by God's word that guarantees my security and supplies in the name of Jesus Christ my Lord. Amen.

As you make these confessions, watch out for what God is doing. He said that you will SEE His word works. See only His word. Nothing else.

DAY EIGHT

Welcome to the eighth day of our confession of faith!

The Passover feast was to commemorate two historic events. First, the night that the death angel passed over Egypt killing the entire first born whose houses had no blood cover. The Israelites came out of Egypt. Second, it reminds us of the night Jesus had His last meal with His disciples before His crucifixion.

The first shows us what God used the second to accomplish for us. Today I am coming out of every bondage in the name of Jesus Christ my Lord. Amen.

In Matt. 26:17-29, we see Jesus observed the Passover. We see the power of confession. From what they were eating, Jesus took bread and blessed it. Matt. 26:26. The word blessed means to speak well of. He spoke to the bread and then to His disciples. ***He said, Take, eat; This is My body.*** Remember, it was bread they were eating. His word changed it to His body. Confession can change bread to body. Your confession can change wine to blood.

It was what Jesus spoke to the bread and wine that transformed them to what He said. You can eat that same bread and drink the wine and still take them as ordinary bread and wine. They would just be bread and wine to you.

You can also agree with Jesus and take them as His body and blood. You decide what they become even after He has spoken to them. This is what confession really is. Jesus spoke to the bread and called it His body. You believe Him, receive not the bread but His body. You eat or chew His body because He said so. To chew or eat is the same word for meditate in Joshua 1:8. So as you confess the word, you are actually chewing or eating His body, His word.

As you eat it, your sins and its consequences are remitted or removed. The impact of confession is that it removes things from you that you can't no matter how otherwise you try.

Now I am ready to eat His body and drink His blood as I make my confessions. I am eating and drinking His word as I make my confessions.

As we continue making our confessions for the rest of the month, I want to remind you of what God said in Numbers 11:18-23. God promised to give you food the whole of this month.

CONFESSION FOR THE MONTH

I believe and declare,

The Lord is my Rock. He is large and solid for me. He can hold me just as I can hold Him. I choose to hold on to Him and His word in the name of Jesus Christ my Lord.

The Lord is my Fortress. He is my stronghold and defense headquarters. As long as I am in Him, no plague can penetrate me. I am safe in Him.

The Lord is my Deliverer. He causes me to escape every assault and attack from the enemy. I am delivered from the plague in the name of Jesus Christ my Lord.

The Lord is my God. I have no other God but Jehovah God. Jehovah Jireh is my God. The El Shaddai is my God. The government is not my God. My God is Supreme and Superior to all. His judgment nullifies all others.

The Lord is my Strength. He empowers, energizes and emboldens me to overcome all tests, trials, troubles, tribulations and temptations. I totally depend on the Lord who strengthens me to overcome this month in the name of Jesus Christ my Lord.

The Lord is my Buckler. He shields me from every dart, arrow and plague shot at me. He wards them off from me. That is why no plague touches me. No sickness or disease or infection or virus touches me. I am safe in Christ Jesus my Lord.

The Lord is the Horn of my Salvation. He saves me and keeps me safe. I am saved and safe in Christ Jesus my Lord.

The Lord is my High Tower. I am impervious and inaccessible to all plagues and pestilence. No evil shall befall me. No plague shall come near me. I have a vantage position. I am not disadvantaged. I have the advantage because the Lord is my High Tower.

The Lord is my Trust. I am secured, insured and assured because I trust in the Lord Jesus Christ. I am not moved by the government or economy or news. I am moved by God's word that guarantees my security and supplies in the name of Jesus Christ my Lord. Amen.

As you make these confessions, watch out for what God is doing. He said that you will SEE His word works. See only His word. Nothing else.

DAY NINE

Welcome to the ninth day of our confession of faith!

How time flies? Do you still remember what you set out to acquire, achieve and accomplish this year? Do you still think you can?

The fact is that you can if you keep at obeying God's simple instruction to hide yourself for a while until the plague ends. Isaiah 26:20-21. While you are hiding in the secret place, you have time to create your world just like God does.

"Go home, my people,

and lock your doors!

Hide yourselves for a little while

until the Lord's anger has passed.

Look! The Lord is coming from heaven

to punish the people of the earth for their sins.

The earth will no longer hide those who have been killed.

They will be brought out for all to see."

Isaiah 26:20-21. New Living Translation

How does God create? In Gen. 1, nine times you will read, ***And God said...*** God creates by speaking what He wants to see. He does nothing until He has spoken it.

Since He created you like Himself, it must be that your most creative capacity is let loosed when you speak what you want to see.

Your confession creates your condition. So whatever it is that you set out to acquire, achieve and accomplish this year, within these 30 days of declarations and confessions, say them into your world. The difference between when you say them and when you see them is just time and chance. Say them so that time and chance will have what you say become what you see.

As we continue making our confessions for the rest of the month, I want to remind you of what God said in Numbers 11:18-23. God promised to give you food the whole of this month.

CONFESSION FOR THE MONTH

I believe and declare,

The Lord is my Rock. He is large and solid for me. He can hold me just as I can hold Him. I choose to hold on to Him and His word in the name of Jesus Christ my Lord.

The Lord is my Fortress. He is my stronghold and defense headquarters. As long as I am in Him, no plague can penetrate me. I am safe in Him.

The Lord is my Deliverer. He causes me to escape every assault and attack from the enemy. I am delivered from the plague in the name of Jesus Christ my Lord.

The Lord is my God. I have no other God but Jehovah God. Jehovah Jireh is my God. The El Shaddai is my God. The government is not my God. My God is Supreme and Superior to all. His judgment nullifies all others.

The Lord is my Strength. He empowers, energizes and emboldens me to overcome all tests, trials, troubles, tribulations and temptations. I totally depend on the Lord who strengthens me to overcome this month in the name of Jesus Christ my Lord.

The Lord is my Buckler. He shields me from every dart, arrow and plague shot at me. He wards them off from me. That is why no plague touches me. No sickness or disease or infection or virus touches me. I am safe in Christ Jesus my Lord.

The Lord is the Horn of my Salvation. He saves me and keeps me safe. I am saved and safe in Christ Jesus my Lord.

The Lord is my High Tower. I am impervious and inaccessible to all plagues and pestilence. No evil shall befall me. No plague shall come near me. I have a vantage position. I am not disadvantaged. I have the advantage because the Lord is my High Tower.

The Lord is my Trust. I am secured, insured and assured because I trust in the Lord Jesus Christ. I am not moved by the government or economy or news. I am moved by God's word that guarantees my security and supplies in the name of Jesus Christ my Lord. Amen.

As you make these confessions, watch out for what God is doing. He said that you will SEE His word works. See only His word. Nothing else.

DAY TEN

Welcome to the tenth day of our confession of faith!

Today, I want to share one fact that can help you kiss doubt and unbelief goodbye.

It is possible for you live your life without a doubt of God's word. Since doubt and unbelief are the results of your own decisions, you need logic and reason to make that decision and stick with it in spite of people pressure or present position.

One logic that has helped me is that I don't use my education or exposure or experience to validate God. They are too fickle and flawed to validate the unseen God who is by far beyond human comprehension. Yes, I do use my existence sometimes. That is just to encourage myself because I am created by a creator. My existence as a created being is proof that I have a Creator who I need to know.

However, the only thing that can validate God is His word. God is Word. John 1:1. He creates His world with His word. John 1:3. Every time God moves or breaths or walks, He does so by speaking. In Gen. 1:2, we see the Holy Spirit moved. How? He was speaking things into existence. In Gen. 2:7, we see God breaths. How? He was speaking into the human form every part you can find. In 2 Tim. 3:16, it tells us that all scripture is God breathed. When God breathes, He is speaking. He is scripting what we call scripture.

"Every Scripture is God-breathed (given by His inspiration) and profitable for instruction, for reproof and conviction of sin, for correction of error and discipline in obedience, [and] for training in righteousness (in holy living, in conformity to God's will in thought, purpose, and action),

So that the man of God may be complete and proficient, well fitted and thoroughly equipped for every good work."

2 Tim 3:16-17. Amplified Version.

Now, allow me to breath like God by speaking scriptures into my world. If you were getting tired by today, you can see that you just can't stop breathing or else you die. As you keep on breathing God's word, you validate God in your life.

As we continue making our confessions for the rest of the month, I want to remind you of what God said in Numbers 11:18-23. God promised to give you food the whole of this month.

CONFESSION FOR THE MONTH

I believe and declare,

The Lord is my Rock. He is large and solid for me. He can hold me just as I can hold Him. I choose to hold on to Him and His word in the name of Jesus Christ my Lord.

The Lord is my Fortress. He is my stronghold and defense headquarters. As long as I am in Him, no plague can penetrate me. I am safe in Him.

The Lord is my Deliverer. He causes me to escape every assault and attack from the enemy. I am delivered from the plague in the name of Jesus Christ my Lord.

The Lord is my God. I have no other God but Jehovah God. Jehovah Jireh is my God. The El Shaddai is my God. The government is not my God. My God is Supreme and Superior to all. His judgment nullifies all others.

The Lord is my Strength. He empowers, energizes and emboldens me to overcome all tests, trials, troubles, tribulations and temptations. I totally depend on the Lord who strengthens me to overcome this month in the name of Jesus Christ my Lord.

The Lord is my Buckler. He shields me from every dart, arrow and plague shot at me. He wards them off from me. That is why no plague touches me. No sickness or disease or infection or virus touches me. I am safe in Christ Jesus my Lord.

The Lord is the Horn of my Salvation. He saves me and keeps me safe. I am saved and safe in Christ Jesus my Lord.

The Lord is my High Tower. I am impervious and inaccessible to all plagues and pestilence. No evil shall befall me. No plague shall come near me. I have a vantage position. I am not disadvantaged. I have the advantage because the Lord is my High Tower.

The Lord is my Trust. I am secured, insured and assured because I trust in the Lord Jesus Christ. I am not moved by the government or economy or news. I am moved by God's word that guarantees my security and supplies in the name of Jesus Christ my Lord. Amen.

As you make these confessions, watch out for what God is doing. He said that you will SEE His word works. See only His word. Nothing else.

DAY ELEVEN

Welcome to the eleventh day of our confession of faith!

What will it take for you to believe God? It's important you solve this question permanently because it will free you for life. The reason why today we believe God when things are going the way we plan or pleasure and the next day we doubt if God exist is because we are yet to answer that question.

In Gen. 2:7, God formed, framed and fashioned man to believe God. God formed man, breathed into his nostrils the breath of life and man became a living being. The literal translation is that man became a believing being. Put in order words, man became alive because he believed God.

The word **believe** is a combination of two words, **be**ing and **alive**. Or be alive. Every time man decides to believe God, he comes alive. When he decides to doubt or disbelieve God, he dies. To doubt hurts. To believe heals and helps.

For man to constantly believe God, he has to constantly confess his belief of God to himself until it is engraved on his form, frame and fashion. Until that belief in God becomes a part of his being he will doubt and disbelieve God at the slightest crisis or conflict. This is why for 30 days we are making the same confession to imprint and implant our belief in God in our form, frame and fashion. If you do it consistently for 30 days, your form, frame and fashion will accept it as your reality.

Now, let us make our confession with more passion because our belief in God is at stake.

As we continue making our confessions for the rest of the month, I want to remind you of what God said in Numbers 11:18-23. God promised to give you food the whole of this month.

CONFESSION FOR THE MONTH

I believe and declare,

The Lord is my Rock. He is large and solid for me. He can hold me just as I can hold Him. I choose to hold on to Him and His word in the name of Jesus Christ my Lord.

The Lord is my Fortress. He is my stronghold and defense headquarters. As long as I am in Him, no plague can penetrate me. I am safe in Him.

The Lord is my Deliverer. He causes me to escape every assault and attack from the enemy. I am delivered from the plague in the name of Jesus Christ my Lord.

The Lord is my God. I have no other God but Jehovah God. Jehovah Jireh is my God. The El Shaddai is my God. The government is not my God. My God is Supreme and Superior to all. His judgment nullifies all others.

The Lord is my Strength. He empowers, energizes and emboldens me to overcome all tests, trials, troubles, tribulations and temptations. I totally depend on the Lord who strengthens me to overcome this month in the name of Jesus Christ my Lord.

The Lord is my Buckler. He shields me from every dart, arrow and plague shot at me. He wards them off from me. That is why no plague touches me. No sickness or disease or infection or virus touches me. I am safe in Christ Jesus my Lord.

The Lord is the Horn of my Salvation. He saves me and keeps me safe. I am saved and safe in Christ Jesus my Lord.

The Lord is my High Tower. I am impervious and inaccessible to all plagues and pestilence. No evil shall befall me. No plague shall come near me. I have a vantage position. I am not disadvantaged. I have the advantage because the Lord is my High Tower.

The Lord is my Trust. I am secured, insured and assured because I trust in the Lord Jesus Christ. I am not moved by the government or economy or news. I am moved by God's word that guarantees my security and supplies in the name of Jesus Christ my Lord. Amen.

As you make these confessions, watch out for what God is doing. He said that you will SEE His word works. See only His word. Nothing else.

DAY TWELVE

Welcome to the twelfth day of our confession of faith!

What a joy to celebrate the chief cornerstone of our Christian faith. Without the resurrection of Jesus Christ from the grave, Christianity would have been like all other religions. Today, Christianity is not a religion but a life giving relationship because Jesus died and rose again.

Mark 16:6 tells us, *He is risen!* Yes, **Jesus Christ is alive!**

What is Christianity? It is the great confession of our faith in Christ Jesus. The killers of Jesus heard Him say several times, *After three days I will rise again.* Matt. 27:63. He founded Christianity on His confession. That makes confession the foundation of Christianity. You can't become a Christian without confession. You must deliberately make your own confession of Christ for you to be saved.

"But what saith it? The word is nigh thee, even in thy mouth, and in thy heart: that is, the word of faith, which we preach;

That if thou shalt confess with thy mouth the Lord Jesus, and shalt believe in thine heart that God hath raised him from the dead, thou shalt be saved.

For with the heart man believeth unto righteousness; and with the mouth confession is made unto salvation."

Rom. 10:8-10.

If His confession had the capacity to raise Him from the dead in spite of all the hordes of hell and military guards positioned to stop Him, confession must be potent.

If a simple confession I made the day I accepted Christ that totally transformed my life 41 years ago, then, confession must be potent to change my present condition.

With this understanding, I am ready to make my confession because I know that my condition will line up with my confession in Jesus name. Amen.

As we continue making our confessions for the rest of the month, I want to remind you of what God said in Numbers 11:18-23. God promised to give you food the whole of this month.

CONFESSION FOR THE MONTH

I believe and declare,

The Lord is my Rock. He is large and solid for me. He can hold me just as I can hold Him. I choose to hold on to Him and His word in the name of Jesus Christ my Lord.

The Lord is my Fortress. He is my stronghold and defense headquarters. As long as I am in Him, no plague can penetrate me. I am safe in Him.

The Lord is my Deliverer. He causes me to escape every assault and attack from the enemy. I am delivered from the plague in the name of Jesus Christ my Lord.

The Lord is my God. I have no other God but Jehovah God. Jehovah Jireh is my God. The El Shaddai is my God. The government is not my God. My God is Supreme and Superior to all. His judgment nullifies all others.

The Lord is my Strength. He empowers, energizes and emboldens me to overcome all tests, trials, troubles, tribulations and temptations. I totally depend on the Lord who strengthens me to overcome this month in the name of Jesus Christ my Lord.

The Lord is my Buckler. He shields me from every dart, arrow and plague shot at me. He wards them off from me. That is why no plague touches me. No sickness or disease or infection or virus touches me. I am safe in Christ Jesus my Lord.

The Lord is the Horn of my Salvation. He saves me and keeps me safe. I am saved and safe in Christ Jesus my Lord.

The Lord is my High Tower. I am impervious and inaccessible to all plagues and pestilence. No evil shall befall me. No plague shall come near me. I have a vantage position. I am not disadvantaged. I have the advantage because the Lord is my High Tower.

The Lord is my Trust. I am secured, insured and assured because I trust in the Lord Jesus Christ. I am not moved by the government or economy or news. I am moved by God's word that guarantees my security and supplies in the name of Jesus Christ my Lord. Amen.

As you make these confessions, watch out for what God is doing. He said that you will SEE His word works. See only His word. Nothing else.

DAY THIRTEEN

Welcome to the thirteenth day of our confession of faith!

The power of the Christian life is unleashed through preaching or proclamation or prophesy or pronouncements. You will never know the tremendous power that you have as a believer in Christ until you start making your confession deliberately and decisively especially in the face of contradictory conditions.

In times like these when you don't know who to call for help or how you will make it through to next month. This is when your confession becomes the only thing you can do to stay alive and afloat.

In Rom. 10:8-10, we see the word is in your heart and mouth. Yes, you have to keep on chewing it until it is painted on your heart as your reality. It is the word of faith which we confess. Those words have the same capacity as divinity to change your condition.

Two parts of your being you must engage to unleash the power of Christ in you: your heart and your mouth. Condition your heart to believe God by speaking what you believe even if you have to die because of what you believe. The resurrection guarantee is that if you die, Jesus Christ will raise you just like He was raised by the Father. You see why confession is potent. What you confess passionately and persistently is what God uses to decide what really happens to you now or next.

I am ready to make my confession even if it is the last food I eat before my next experience. My confession decides my condition.

As we continue making our confessions for the rest of the month, I want to remind you of what God said in Numbers 11:18-23. God promised to give you food the whole of this month.

CONFESSION FOR THE MONTH

I believe and declare,

The Lord is my Rock. He is large and solid for me. He can hold me just as I can hold Him. I choose to hold on to Him and His word in the name of Jesus Christ my Lord.

The Lord is my Fortress. He is my stronghold and defense headquarters. As long as I am in Him, no plague can penetrate me. I am safe in Him.

The Lord is my Deliverer. He causes me to escape every assault and attack from the enemy. I am delivered from the plague in the name of Jesus Christ my Lord.

The Lord is my God. I have no other God but Jehovah God. Jehovah Jireh is my God. The El Shaddai is my God. The government is not my God. My God is Supreme and Superior to all. His judgment nullifies all others.

The Lord is my Strength. He empowers, energizes and emboldens me to overcome all tests, trials, troubles, tribulations and temptations. I totally depend on the Lord who strengthens me to overcome this month in the name of Jesus Christ my Lord.

The Lord is my Buckler. He shields me from every dart, arrow and plague shot at me. He wards them off from me. That is why no plague touches me. No sickness or disease or infection or virus touches me. I am safe in Christ Jesus my Lord.

The Lord is the Horn of my Salvation. He saves me and keeps me safe. I am saved and safe in Christ Jesus my Lord.

The Lord is my High Tower. I am impervious and inaccessible to all plagues and pestilence. No evil shall befall me. No plague shall come near me. I have a vantage position. I am not disadvantaged. I have the advantage because the Lord is my High Tower.

The Lord is my Trust. I am secured, insured and assured because I trust in the Lord Jesus Christ. I am not moved by the government or economy or news. I am moved by God's word that guarantees my security and supplies in the name of Jesus Christ my Lord. Amen.

As you make these confessions, watch out for what God is doing. He said that you will SEE His word works. See only His word. Nothing else.

DAY FOURTEEN

Welcome to the fourteenth day of our confession of faith!

In Luke 22:19, Jesus took bread, gave thanks, broke it and gave it to His disciples saying, ***This is my body which is given for you: this do in remembrance of me.*** This scripture forms the practice of the Holy Communion on a daily or weekly basis.

Jesus knows the human form, frame and fashion with a notable ability to forget what it should remember and remember what it should forget. 250 times in the Bible, God calls His people to remember. One reason we have to take the communion daily is to help us remember Him. It is for this same reason we have to make our confession on a daily basis so we can remember Him.

If Adam in his perfect state could forget what God told him about the forbidden fruit, he would probably not have bowed to the pressure or pleasure of his wife to eat the forbidden fruit when she gave it to him. If Joseph and Mary can forget their young son Jesus only to discover that he was not in their company after three days, then, you can forget that God can provide for you in times like these.

You can see why God gave us His promise and commanded us to say it to ourselves daily until we see His word come to pass just as He said. Now I need to make my confession to remember Him for who He is to me until it becomes my reality.

As we continue making our confessions for the rest of the month, I want to remind you of what God said in Numbers 11:18-23. God promised to give you food the whole of this month.

CONFESSION FOR THE MONTH

I believe and declare,

The Lord is my Rock. He is large and solid for me. He can hold me just as I can hold Him. I choose to hold on to Him and His word in the name of Jesus Christ my Lord.

The Lord is my Fortress. He is my stronghold and defense headquarters. As long as I am in Him, no plague can penetrate me. I am safe in Him.

The Lord is my Deliverer. He causes me to escape every assault and attack from the enemy. I am delivered from the plague in the name of Jesus Christ my Lord.

The Lord is my God. I have no other God but Jehovah God. Jehovah Jireh is my God. The El Shaddai is my God. The government is not my God. My God is Supreme and Superior to all. His judgment nullifies all others.

The Lord is my Strength. He empowers, energizes and emboldens me to overcome all tests, trials, troubles, tribulations and temptations. I totally depend on the Lord who strengthens me to overcome this month in the name of Jesus Christ my Lord.

The Lord is my Buckler. He shields me from every dart, arrow and plague shot at me. He wards them off from me. That is why no plague touches me. No sickness or disease or infection or virus touches me. I am safe in Christ Jesus my Lord.

The Lord is the Horn of my Salvation. He saves me and keeps me safe. I am saved and safe in Christ Jesus my Lord.

The Lord is my High Tower. I am impervious and inaccessible to all plagues and pestilence. No evil shall befall me. No plague shall come near me. I have a vantage position. I am not disadvantaged. I have the advantage because the Lord is my High Tower.

The Lord is my Trust. I am secured, insured and assured because I trust in the Lord Jesus Christ. I am not moved by the government or economy or news. I am moved

by God's word that guarantees my security and supplies in the name of Jesus Christ
my Lord. Amen.

As you make these confessions, watch out for what God is doing. He said that you
will SEE His word works. See only His word. Nothing else.

DAY FIFTEEN

Welcome to the fifteenth day of our confession of faith!

God does nothing except by His word because He is the word. All things were made by the word, the spoken word. Without the spoken word, nothing manifest. That right there is the power of confession. Nothing manifest until it is spoken.

"In the beginning was the Word, and the Word was with God, and the Word was God.

The same was in the beginning with God.

All things were made by him; and without him was not any thing made that was made."

John 1:1-3.

Whatever you desire to see manifest in your world, you must deliberately speak them into existence. Whatever you see right now, you spoke them sometime in your past. Whatever you will see tomorrow, you have a responsibility to speak them today. Say what you want to see. See only what you have said. I choose to speak God's word until I see it.

As we continue making our confessions for the rest of the month, I want to remind you of what God said in Numbers 11:18-23. God promised to give you food the whole of this month.

CONFESSION FOR THE MONTH

I believe and declare,

The Lord is my Rock. He is large and solid for me. He can hold me just as I can hold Him. I choose to hold on to Him and His word in the name of Jesus Christ my Lord.

The Lord is my Fortress. He is my stronghold and defense headquarters. As long as I am in Him, no plague can penetrate me. I am safe in Him.

The Lord is my Deliverer. He causes me to escape every assault and attack from the enemy. I am delivered from the plague in the name of Jesus Christ my Lord.

The Lord is my God. I have no other God but Jehovah God. Jehovah Jireh is my God. The El Shaddai is my God. The government is not my God. My God is Supreme and Superior to all. His judgment nullifies all others.

The Lord is my Strength. He empowers, energizes and emboldens me to overcome all tests, trials, troubles, tribulations and temptations. I totally depend on the Lord who strengthens me to overcome this month in the name of Jesus Christ my Lord.

The Lord is my Buckler. He shields me from every dart, arrow and plague shot at me. He wards them off from me. That is why no plague touches me. No sickness or disease or infection or virus touches me. I am safe in Christ Jesus my Lord.

The Lord is the Horn of my Salvation. He saves me and keeps me safe. I am saved and safe in Christ Jesus my Lord.

The Lord is my High Tower. I am impervious and inaccessible to all plagues and pestilence. No evil shall befall me. No plague shall come near me. I have a vantage position. I am not disadvantaged. I have the advantage because the Lord is my High Tower.

The Lord is my Trust. I am secured, insured and assured because I trust in the Lord Jesus Christ. I am not moved by the government or economy or news. I am moved by God's word that guarantees my security and supplies in the name of Jesus Christ my Lord. Amen.

As you make these confessions, watch out for what God is doing. He said that you will SEE His word works. See only His word. Nothing else.

DAY SIXTEEN

Welcome to the sixteenth day of our confession of faith!

Man was created by God to speak. In Gen. 2:7, God formed, framed and fashioned man from the dust of the ground. Man could have been relegated to the ground permanently if not for what God did to him. God breathed into his nostrils the breath of life and man became a living being. Man stood up from the ground.

"God formed Man out of dirt from the ground and blew into his nostrils the breath of life. The Man came alive — a living soul!"

Gen 2:7. The Message Version.

When God breathed into man, it was not the act of inhaling and exhaling air. God doesn't inhale or exhale. When God breaths, He is speaking. He literally spoke into man's form what gives man life. When the man stood up from the ground, he began to speak what God spoke to him. No wonder he could name God's creation exactly what God thought to name them.

"And out of the ground the Lord God formed every beast of the field, and every fowl of the air; and brought them unto Adam to see what he would call them: and whatsoever Adam called every living creature, that was the name thereof.

And Adam gave names to all cattle, and to the fowl of the air, and to every beast of the field; but for Adam there was not found an help meet for him."

Gen. 2:19-20.

Now you can see what shut man up from the ground. It was what God spoke to the man that the man spoke to God and himself. Yes, confession is speaking to God and yourself what God has spoken to you. It is not speaking what the government or economy or news media are saying. They have a right to say whatever they have to say just as you have. You can choose to keep on saying what they are saying or you can choose to keep on saying what God has said.

You choose your pick or pick your choice and stick with it until the end. I choose to say what God has said. Now I am ready to speak what God said to me because I know it will lift me up from the ground to glory.

As we continue making our confessions for the rest of the month, I want to remind you of what God said in Numbers 11:18-23. God promised to give you food the whole of this month.

CONFESSION FOR THE MONTH

I believe and declare,

The Lord is my Rock. He is large and solid for me. He can hold me just as I can hold Him. I choose to hold on to Him and His word in the name of Jesus Christ my Lord.

The Lord is my Fortress. He is my stronghold and defense headquarters. As long as I am in Him, no plague can penetrate me. I am safe in Him.

The Lord is my Deliverer. He causes me to escape every assault and attack from the enemy. I am delivered from the plague in the name of Jesus Christ my Lord.

The Lord is my God. I have no other God but Jehovah God. Jehovah Jireh is my God. The El Shaddai is my God. The government is not my God. My God is Supreme and Superior to all. His judgment nullifies all others.

The Lord is my Strength. He empowers, energizes and emboldens me to overcome all tests, trials, troubles, tribulations and temptations. I totally depend on the Lord who strengthens me to overcome this month in the name of Jesus Christ my Lord.

The Lord is my Buckler. He shields me from every dart, arrow and plague shot at me. He wards them off from me. That is why no plague touches me. No sickness or disease or infection or virus touches me. I am safe in Christ Jesus my Lord.

The Lord is the Horn of my Salvation. He saves me and keeps me safe. I am saved and safe in Christ Jesus my Lord.

The Lord is my High Tower. I am impervious and inaccessible to all plagues and pestilence. No evil shall befall me. No plague shall come near me. I have a vantage position. I am not disadvantaged. I have the advantage because the Lord is my High Tower.

The Lord is my Trust. I am secured, insured and assured because I trust in the Lord Jesus Christ. I am not moved by the government or economy or news. I am moved by God's word that guarantees my security and supplies in the name of Jesus Christ my Lord. Amen.

As you make these confessions, watch out for what God is doing. He said that you will SEE His word works. See only His word. Nothing else.

DAY SEVENTEEN

Welcome to the seventeenth day of our confession of faith!

Looking at Gen. 2:7, the way God formed, framed and fashioned man is such that man must speak himself up from the ground up. I am responsible for speaking myself up from the ground up. You are responsible for speaking yourself from the ground up. Nobody will do it for you.

This is God's pattern. God speaks to man. Man speaks what God spoke to him. It is God's word that man speaks that decides what happens to man.

Your environment or economy doesn't decide what happens to you. In fact, what's outside is not powerful enough to change you until you suck it in and spill it out. Yes, this is the secret to changes in man. Suck in God's breath or word and spit it out to your environment.

What has God spoken to you about yourself, your condition and even the present global condition? Suck in what He has spoken to you. Eat it and be ready to spit it out at every opportunity. Be mindful of the fact that we all don't hear from God. So don't get distracted by what others are saying. They have a right to say what they say just as you have a right to say what you say. This is your human right. Use it or lose it.

Thank God I heard a clear word from God for this time and that is exactly what I am declaring. Now, I am ready to make my confession because my confession creates my condition.

As we continue making our confessions for the rest of the month, I want to remind you of what God said in Numbers 11:18-23. God promised to give you food the whole of this month.

CONFESSION FOR THE MONTH

I believe and declare,

The Lord is my Rock. He is large and solid for me. He can hold me just as I can hold Him. I choose to hold on to Him and His word in the name of Jesus Christ my Lord.

The Lord is my Fortress. He is my stronghold and defense headquarters. As long as I am in Him, no plague can penetrate me. I am safe in Him.

The Lord is my Deliverer. He causes me to escape every assault and attack from the enemy. I am delivered from the plague in the name of Jesus Christ my Lord.

The Lord is my God. I have no other God but Jehovah God. Jehovah Jireh is my God. The El Shaddai is my God. The government is not my God. My God is Supreme and Superior to all. His judgment nullifies all others.

The Lord is my Strength. He empowers, energizes and emboldens me to overcome all tests, trials, troubles, tribulations and temptations. I totally depend on the Lord who strengthens me to overcome this month in the name of Jesus Christ my Lord.

The Lord is my Buckler. He shields me from every dart, arrow and plague shot at me. He wards them off from me. That is why no plague touches me. No sickness or disease or infection or virus touches me. I am safe in Christ Jesus my Lord.

The Lord is the Horn of my Salvation. He saves me and keeps me safe. I am saved and safe in Christ Jesus my Lord.

The Lord is my High Tower. I am impervious and inaccessible to all plagues and pestilence. No evil shall befall me. No plague shall come near me. I have a vantage position. I am not disadvantaged. I have the advantage because the Lord is my High Tower.

The Lord is my Trust. I am secured, insured and assured because I trust in the Lord Jesus Christ. I am not moved by the government or economy or news. I am moved by God's word that guarantees my security and supplies in the name of Jesus Christ my Lord. Amen.

As you make these confessions, watch out for what God is doing. He said that you will SEE His word works. See only His word. Nothing else.

DAY EIGHTEEN

Welcome to the eighteenth day of our confession of faith!

Of the three rich resources available to everyone: words, works and wealth, words happen to be the mother of them. This is so because God the Creator is Word. John 1:1. Everything created by God and man are the results of words. Nothing exists without words. Words make things real. Your works, the work of your hands and wealth are products of words.

This is so because just as God is Word even so man is a word being. God spoke man into existence in Gen. 1:26-28. God formed, framed and fashioned man by His breath, inspired words in Gen. 2:7. That is why if man must produce, he must be inspired by someone speaking life giving words into his being.

No matter how dull or dumb or dead a man is to you, he can come alive when he hears someone who speaks into his being life giving words. Inspired words are like electric current that can wake up even the dead at high voltage. Inspired or spoken words are currents with high voltage. They can raise the dead to life. They can raise the poor to prosperity. They can raise you from the backstage to the front lines. They can change crisis and chaos to conquest. They can cure faster than any medicine or vaccine.

Since no one can speak the kinds of inspired words you really need to rise out of the pit to your palace better than you that is why God gave you a mouth to move your life to any height or depth. You are the best prophet of your life. Now you can prophesy what you want to see by making your confession with such intensity and passion like never before.

As we continue making our confessions for the rest of the month, I want to remind you of what God said in Numbers 11:18-23. God promised to give you food the whole of this month.

CONFESSION FOR THE MONTH

I believe and declare,

The Lord is my Rock. He is large and solid for me. He can hold me just as I can hold Him. I choose to hold on to Him and His word in the name of Jesus Christ my Lord.

The Lord is my Fortress. He is my stronghold and defense headquarters. As long as I am in Him, no plague can penetrate me. I am safe in Him.

The Lord is my Deliverer. He causes me to escape every assault and attack from the enemy. I am delivered from the plague in the name of Jesus Christ my Lord.

The Lord is my God. I have no other God but Jehovah God. Jehovah Jireh is my God. The El Shaddai is my God. The government is not my God. My God is Supreme and Superior to all. His judgment nullifies all others.

The Lord is my Strength. He empowers, energizes and emboldens me to overcome all tests, trials, troubles, tribulations and temptations. I totally depend on the Lord who strengthens me to overcome this month in the name of Jesus Christ my Lord.

The Lord is my Buckler. He shields me from every dart, arrow and plague shot at me. He wards them off from me. That is why no plague touches me. No sickness or disease or infection or virus touches me. I am safe in Christ Jesus my Lord.

The Lord is the Horn of my Salvation. He saves me and keeps me safe. I am saved and safe in Christ Jesus my Lord.

The Lord is my High Tower. I am impervious and inaccessible to all plagues and pestilence. No evil shall befall me. No plague shall come near me. I have a vantage position. I am not disadvantaged. I have the advantage because the Lord is my High Tower.

The Lord is my Trust. I am secured, insured and assured because I trust in the Lord Jesus Christ. I am not moved by the government or economy or news. I am moved by God's word that guarantees my security and supplies in the name of Jesus Christ my Lord. Amen.

As you make these confessions, watch out for what God is doing. He said that you will SEE His word works. See only His word. Nothing else.

DAY NINETEEN

Welcome to the nineteenth day of our confession of faith!

It is evident that words are the most powerful creative force God gave man. God planned and designed man by His word. The law of design states that everything designed is sustained by its source. The designer is the only one who can guarantee the sustenance of his design.

"And God said, Let us make man in our image, after our likeness: and let them have dominion over the fish of the sea, and over the fowl of the air, and over the cattle, and over all the earth, and over every creeping thing that creepeth upon the earth."

Gen. 1:26.

Man was designed by God and can only be sustained by God. Since God essentially is Word, man was designed by the Word of God and can only be sustained by the word of God. This is the reason why every day for any man to survive or succeed or be sustained, he must make it a daily habit to look at God's word. By looking or reading or meditating or studying or memorizing or confessing God's word, he is looking at God face to face. It is this face to face encounter with God that radically transforms man to look exactly like how God designed him to look.

From the original design, God wants man to look like Him by looking at Him. The image or reflection of God is a face to face encounter. That is what we see in Gen. 2:7 as God faces man eye to eye, nose to nose, man came alive. Man can only become by having a face to face encounter with God.

“But we all, with open face beholding as in a glass the glory of the Lord, are changed into the same image from glory to glory, even as by the Spirit of the Lord.”

2 Cor. 3:18.

The key word there is, **beholding**, a present continuous practice. You don't look at Him yesterday and think you will be fine today from yesterday. The fact is that, by today, you have forgotten what He looked like yesterday. We forget daily so easily. That is why we fall, fail and fumble because we forget.

Every day, I need to see His face. I need to hear His voice. I need to romance Him. The glory of that encounter carries me for the day. Just the same way my confession carries me for the day. Now I need to make my confession for today because I really need Him today.

As we continue making our confessions for the rest of the month, I want to remind you of what God said in Numbers 11:18-23. God promised to give you food the whole of this month.

CONFESSION FOR THE MONTH

I believe and declare,

The Lord is my Rock. He is large and solid for me. He can hold me just as I can hold Him. I choose to hold on to Him and His word in the name of Jesus Christ my Lord.

The Lord is my Fortress. He is my stronghold and defense headquarters. As long as I am in Him, no plague can penetrate me. I am safe in Him.

The Lord is my Deliverer. He causes me to escape every assault and attack from the enemy. I am delivered from the plague in the name of Jesus Christ my Lord.

The Lord is my God. I have no other God but Jehovah God. Jehovah Jireh is my God. The El Shaddai is my God. The government is not my God. My God is Supreme and Superior to all. His judgment nullifies all others.

The Lord is my Strength. He empowers, energizes and emboldens me to overcome all tests, trials, troubles, tribulations and temptations. I totally depend on the Lord who strengthens me to overcome this month in the name of Jesus Christ my Lord.

The Lord is my Buckler. He shields me from every dart, arrow and plague shot at me. He wards them off from me. That is why no plague touches me. No sickness or disease or infection or virus touches me. I am safe in Christ Jesus my Lord.

The Lord is the Horn of my Salvation. He saves me and keeps me safe. I am saved and safe in Christ Jesus my Lord.

The Lord is my High Tower. I am impervious and inaccessible to all plagues and pestilence. No evil shall befall me. No plague shall come near me. I have a vantage position. I am not disadvantaged. I have the advantage because the Lord is my High Tower.

The Lord is my Trust. I am secured, insured and assured because I trust in the Lord Jesus Christ. I am not moved by the government or economy or news. I am moved by God's word that guarantees my security and supplies in the name of Jesus Christ my Lord. Amen.

As you make these confessions, watch out for what God is doing. He said that you will SEE His word works. See only His word. Nothing else.

DAY TWENTY

Welcome to the twentieth day of our confession of faith!

How would you like to have a face to face encounter with God? I want that every day of my life. One man who had face to face encounter with God was Moses.

"And there arose not a prophet since in Israel like unto Moses, whom the Lord knew face to face."

Deut. 34:10.

Although, God wanted all Israel to have that kind of relationship but they changed their minds after only one encounter.

Interestingly, this is the kind of relationship God created man for. Of all of God's creation, man is the only creation of God that God communicates with face to face. Even angels don't have this privilege. In Gen. 1:26, God created man to look like God by looking at God. The pleasure He derives from man looking at Him is indescribable. You can now understand why you like looking at some people.

Later, you see that same interaction between God and man in Gen. 2:7 as He molds man and breaths into man all of His essence and divinity. His hands and face were all involved in the making of man. No wonder man likes to be touched and taken notice of. From that interaction and intercourse, I see that there are two practices that bring us face to face with God. They are communion and confession.

"And when He had given thanks, He broke [it] and said, Take, eat. This is My body, which is broken for you. Do this to call Me [affectionately] to remembrance."

1 Cor 11:24. Amplified Version.

Every time you take the communion, Jesus said that you do it to remember Him. You can't take communion without confession. Both go together to bring the freshness of His presence. Every time you take communion and make your confession, you are having a face to face encounter with God.

Now I am ready to have a face to face encounter with the eternal God who is my refuge.

As we continue making our confessions for the rest of the month, I want to remind you of what God said in Numbers 11:18-23. God promised to give you food the whole of this month.

CONFESSION FOR THE MONTH

I believe and declare,

The Lord is my Rock. He is large and solid for me. He can hold me just as I can hold Him. I choose to hold on to Him and His word in the name of Jesus Christ my Lord.

The Lord is my Fortress. He is my stronghold and defense headquarters. As long as I am in Him, no plague can penetrate me. I am safe in Him.

The Lord is my Deliverer. He causes me to escape every assault and attack from the enemy. I am delivered from the plague in the name of Jesus Christ my Lord.

The Lord is my God. I have no other God but Jehovah God. Jehovah Jireh is my God. The El Shaddai is my God. The government is not my God. My God is Supreme and Superior to all. His judgment nullifies all others.

The Lord is my Strength. He empowers, energizes and emboldens me to overcome all tests, trials, troubles, tribulations and temptations. I totally depend on the Lord who strengthens me to overcome this month in the name of Jesus Christ my Lord.

The Lord is my Buckler. He shields me from every dart, arrow and plague shot at me. He wards them off from me. That is why no plague touches me. No sickness or disease or infection or virus touches me. I am safe in Christ Jesus my Lord.

The Lord is the Horn of my Salvation. He saves me and keeps me safe. I am saved and safe in Christ Jesus my Lord.

The Lord is my High Tower. I am impervious and inaccessible to all plagues and pestilence. No evil shall befall me. No plague shall come near me. I have a vantage position. I am not disadvantaged. I have the advantage because the Lord is my High Tower.

The Lord is my Trust. I am secured, insured and assured because I trust in the Lord Jesus Christ. I am not moved by the government or economy or news. I am moved by God's word that guarantees my security and supplies in the name of Jesus Christ my Lord. Amen.

As you make these confessions, watch out for what God is doing. He said that you will SEE His word works. See only His word. Nothing else.

DAY TWENTY-ONE

Welcome to the twenty first day of our confession of faith!

God is a God of pattern. He sets a pattern for His intern, man, from the beginning. In Gen. 1:1, He created everything in heaven and earth. To show man His pattern the power of communion and confession, in Gen. 1:2, He didn't just set off to change the state of the earth until He had had communion as we see the Holy Spirit moving upon the face of the waters. The water there is God Himself. His face was etched in the waters.

The Holy Spirit was actually romancing the face of God. From that intercourse and communion, the word came forth in Gen. 1:3. ***And God said***, is the product of communion.

Before you make your confession, make sure you have communion with Him. The strength or force in confession is generated from communion with God. Anyone can say anything and amounts to nothing. However, if you speak from the place of fellowship and communion, your words are not just your words. They are the words of those you have communion with.

No wonder, after God had breathed into man so much word, when God told man to name His creation, everything man said was exactly what God had in mind. Gen. 2:19. The fact is that, man gave names to God's creation based on what God spoke to him in Gen. 2:7. That is exactly what confession is, saying what God has said.

As we continue making our confessions for the rest of the month, I want to remind you of what God said in Numbers 11:18-23. God promised to give you food the whole of this month.

CONFESSION FOR THE MONTH

I believe and declare,

The Lord is my Rock. He is large and solid for me. He can hold me just as I can hold Him. I choose to hold on to Him and His word in the name of Jesus Christ my Lord.

The Lord is my Fortress. He is my stronghold and defense headquarters. As long as I am in Him, no plague can penetrate me. I am safe in Him.

The Lord is my Deliverer. He causes me to escape every assault and attack from the enemy. I am delivered from the plague in the name of Jesus Christ my Lord.

The Lord is my God. I have no other God but Jehovah God. Jehovah Jireh is my God. The El Shaddai is my God. The government is not my God. My God is Supreme and Superior to all. His judgment nullifies all others.

The Lord is my Strength. He empowers, energizes and emboldens me to overcome all tests, trials, troubles, tribulations and temptations. I totally depend on the Lord who strengthens me to overcome this month in the name of Jesus Christ my Lord.

The Lord is my Buckler. He shields me from every dart, arrow and plague shot at me. He wards them off from me. That is why no plague touches me. No sickness or disease or infection or virus touches me. I am safe in Christ Jesus my Lord.

The Lord is the Horn of my Salvation. He saves me and keeps me safe. I am saved and safe in Christ Jesus my Lord.

The Lord is my High Tower. I am impervious and inaccessible to all plagues and pestilence. No evil shall befall me. No plague shall come near me. I have a vantage position. I am not disadvantaged. I have the advantage because the Lord is my High Tower.

The Lord is my Trust. I am secured, insured and assured because I trust in the Lord Jesus Christ. I am not moved by the government or economy or news. I am moved

by God's word that guarantees my security and supplies in the name of Jesus Christ my Lord. Amen.

As you make these confessions, watch out for what God is doing. He said that you will SEE His word works. See only His word. Nothing else.

DAY TWENTY-TWO

Welcome to the twenty second day of our confession of faith!

Name. Only the Creator has the ability, authority and audacity to name His creation. No creature can name another. Only God has the monopoly to name. Of all of God's creation, only man did God bestow the power and privilege to name His creation in Gen. 2:19.

To name is not so easy because a name invokes the potential and possibility that makes the name powerful or productive. To name is a display of wisdom at its peak. You can't just name something or someone or someplace Chakwinta and be cool because it's meaninglessness only reveals your emptiness and powerlessness. Plato said that the wisest man that ever lived is the one who gave names to God's creation. Naming is an expression of superior intelligence or wisdom.

To name is to call forth what you want to see. It may not be there right now but you can call it forth by naming it. There is a huge difference between being an expert and making impact. Experts say what they see. Those who make impact say what they want to see. An expert looked at Gen. 1:2 and all they saw and said were chaos. God looked at the same earth and called forth light to replace the darkness.

Experts may have all the facts and figures to prove they are right. However, no condition is as they always appear. Experts can be wrong. I have been in London several times when the experts have given four different weather forecasts in one day and they were all wrong. Every Londoner knows this.

Why does God let this happen? Why does He allow the forecast of highly esteemed people to fail? Why does He allow even prophets to fail sometimes? Psalm 118:11. All men are liars. Rom. 3:4, Let God be true but every man a liar. Only God is true. Only God's word is the truth. Any name people have called you or your condition or the present condition is a lie. Don't believe them. Choose to believe God and declare His word instead.

"No, indeed! God tells the truth, even if everyone else is a liar. The Scriptures say about God, "Your words will be proven true, and in court you will win your case."

Rom. 3:4. Contemporary English Version.

Since I have been given the ability, authority and audacity to name myself, my situation and future, I choose to name it in line with what God has named it. Remember, it was what God spoke to Adam in Gen. 2:7 that Adam named God's creation in Gen. 2:19 and it was so. If I call forth what God has spoken to me in this chaotic world that is exactly what I will see in the days, weeks, months and years ahead. I choose to believe and declare what God has said.

As we continue making our confessions for the rest of the month, I want to remind you of what God said in Numbers 11:18-23. God promised to give you food the whole of this month.

CONFESSION FOR THE MONTH

I believe and declare,

The Lord is my Rock. He is large and solid for me. He can hold me just as I can hold Him. I choose to hold on to Him and His word in the name of Jesus Christ my Lord.

The Lord is my Fortress. He is my stronghold and defense headquarters. As long as I am in Him, no plague can penetrate me. I am safe in Him.

The Lord is my Deliverer. He causes me to escape every assault and attack from the enemy. I am delivered from the plague in the name of Jesus Christ my Lord.

The Lord is my God. I have no other God but Jehovah God. Jehovah Jireh is my God. The El Shaddai is my God. The government is not my God. My God is Supreme and Superior to all. His judgment nullifies all others.

The Lord is my Strength. He empowers, energizes and emboldens me to overcome all tests, trials, troubles, tribulations and temptations. I totally depend on the Lord who strengthens me to overcome this month in the name of Jesus Christ my Lord.

The Lord is my Buckler. He shields me from every dart, arrow and plague shot at me. He wards them off from me. That is why no plague touches me. No sickness or disease or infection or virus touches me. I am safe in Christ Jesus my Lord.

The Lord is the Horn of my Salvation. He saves me and keeps me safe. I am saved and safe in Christ Jesus my Lord.

The Lord is my High Tower. I am impervious and inaccessible to all plagues and pestilence. No evil shall befall me. No plague shall come near me. I have a vantage position. I am not disadvantaged. I have the advantage because the Lord is my High Tower.

The Lord is my Trust. I am secured, insured and assured because I trust in the Lord Jesus Christ. I am not moved by the government or economy or news. I am moved by God's word that guarantees my security and supplies in the name of Jesus Christ my Lord. Amen.

As you make these confessions, watch out for what God is doing. He said that you will SEE His word works. See only His word. Nothing else.

DAY TWENTY-THREE

Welcome to the twenty third day of our confession of faith!

Looking at Gen. 2:19-20, we see how much God trust man with the ability, authority and audacity to name His creation. That is awesome power and privilege.

Interestingly, man didn't disappoint God. When God trust you, never use your own mouth to trash yourself. Even if people try to trash you, refuse to accept it. Your Creator believes in you. If mere mortals refuse to believe in you, don't take them seriously because very soon they will not be around.

Look at what Adam did and I know that God trust you to do the same. God formed, framed and fashioned every beast and birds. He brought them to the man and told him, now, you give them names. Interestingly, whatever name Adam called them that was the exact same name God intended for them. Adam and God said the same thing.

Now, it is your turn. What has God placed before you to name? The year is still ahead of you. Name it. Your whole life and family are ahead of you. Name them. Your finances are before you. They say there is recession. They say there is a pandemic. What are you saying? Refuse to join the mob. Stand out to be different.

Since I have been trusted by God with the ability, authority and audacity to name myself, my condition and future, I am going to call it what God has said to me. You say your own. I say my own.

As we continue making our confessions for the rest of the month, I want to remind you of what God said in Numbers 11:18-23. God promised to give you food the whole of this month.

CONFESSION FOR THE MONTH

I believe and declare,

The Lord is my Rock. He is large and solid for me. He can hold me just as I can hold Him. I choose to hold on to Him and His word in the name of Jesus Christ my Lord.

The Lord is my Fortress. He is my stronghold and defense headquarters. As long as I am in Him, no plague can penetrate me. I am safe in Him.

The Lord is my Deliverer. He causes me to escape every assault and attack from the enemy. I am delivered from the plague in the name of Jesus Christ my Lord.

The Lord is my God. I have no other God but Jehovah God. Jehovah Jireh is my God. The El Shaddai is my God. The government is not my God. My God is Supreme and Superior to all. His judgment nullifies all others.

The Lord is my Strength. He empowers, energizes and emboldens me to overcome all tests, trials, troubles, tribulations and temptations. I totally depend on the Lord who strengthens me to overcome this month in the name of Jesus Christ my Lord.

The Lord is my Buckler. He shields me from every dart, arrow and plague shot at me. He wards them off from me. That is why no plague touches me. No sickness or disease or infection or virus touches me. I am safe in Christ Jesus my Lord.

The Lord is the Horn of my Salvation. He saves me and keeps me safe. I am saved and safe in Christ Jesus my Lord.

The Lord is my High Tower. I am impervious and inaccessible to all plagues and pestilence. No evil shall befall me. No plague shall come near me. I have a vantage position. I am not disadvantaged. I have the advantage because the Lord is my High Tower.

The Lord is my Trust. I am secured, insured and assured because I trust in the Lord Jesus Christ. I am not moved by the government or economy or news. I am moved

by God's word that guarantees my security and supplies in the name of Jesus Christ my Lord. Amen.

As you make these confessions, watch out for what God is doing. He said that you will SEE His word works. See only His word. Nothing else.

DAY TWENTY-FOUR

Welcome to the twenty fourth day of our confession of faith!

Nothing works in Christianity until God and someone say the same thing. If you are a Christian and you really want to enjoy the Christian life, you have to decide daily to hear what God says and deliberately say it to yourself, your situation and someone else. In fact, it is what God says that you say consistently that really makes you different from all others and make you a God kind.

In Rom. 10:6-8, we see that the righteousness of the Christian life speaks. It doesn't speak about going to heaven to bring down Christ to do for us what He has commanded us to do. He doesn't speak about going to the deep to look for Christ as if He is not real. Instead, it speaks God's word relevant to the situation. It speaks what should be.

"But the salvation that comes through faith says, "You don't need to search the heavens to find Christ and bring him down to help you," and,

"You don't need to go among the dead to bring Christ back to life again."

For salvation that comes from trusting Christ-which is what we preach-is already within easy reach of each of us; in fact, it is as near as our own hearts and mouths."

Rom. 10:6-8. The Living Bible.

This is how powerful the Christ life is. It has the capacity to change your life, situation and others. However, this tremendous power is only manifest when spoken. You can preach or proclaim or prophesy it. You can say or sing or speak it. You must be deliberate about it until you see it.

How long it takes to manifest is not your department. Your department is to speak it. His department is to make it happen. He gave us the easy part of the job. Incidentally, it is the ease in it that makes us despise it. We think that you can't just move a mountain just because you said it. So we have to get our bulldozers and heavy machines to make it happen. Well, some of us have learned from experience that His way is easy if we stick with it. You can choose His way or your way. I choose His way and that is why I am making these confessions daily.

As we continue making our confessions for the rest of the month, I want to remind you of what God said in Numbers 11:18-23. God promised to give you food the whole of this month.

CONFESSION FOR THE MONTH

I believe and declare,

The Lord is my Rock. He is large and solid for me. He can hold me just as I can hold Him. I choose to hold on to Him and His word in the name of Jesus Christ my Lord.

The Lord is my Fortress. He is my stronghold and defense headquarters. As long as I am in Him, no plague can penetrate me. I am safe in Him.

The Lord is my Deliverer. He causes me to escape every assault and attack from the enemy. I am delivered from the plague in the name of Jesus Christ my Lord.

The Lord is my God. I have no other God but Jehovah God. Jehovah Jireh is my God. The El Shaddai is my God. The government is not my God. My God is Supreme and Superior to all. His judgment nullifies all others.

The Lord is my Strength. He empowers, energizes and emboldens me to overcome all tests, trials, troubles, tribulations and temptations. I totally depend on the Lord who strengthens me to overcome this month in the name of Jesus Christ my Lord.

The Lord is my Buckler. He shields me from every dart, arrow and plague shot at me. He wards them off from me. That is why no plague touches me. No sickness or disease or infection or virus touches me. I am safe in Christ Jesus my Lord.

The Lord is the Horn of my Salvation. He saves me and keeps me safe. I am saved and safe in Christ Jesus my Lord.

The Lord is my High Tower. I am impervious and inaccessible to all plagues and pestilence. No evil shall befall me. No plague shall come near me. I have a vantage position. I am not disadvantaged. I have the advantage because the Lord is my High Tower.

The Lord is my Trust. I am secured, insured and assured because I trust in the Lord Jesus Christ. I am not moved by the government or economy or news. I am moved by God's word that guarantees my security and supplies in the name of Jesus Christ my Lord. Amen.

As you make these confessions, watch out for what God is doing. He said that you will SEE His word works. See only His word. Nothing else.

<h1 style="text-align:center">DAY TWENTY-FIVE</h1>

Welcome to the twenty fifth day of our confession of faith!

The Christian life is a life of faith. It is a life lived by faith. The just will always live by faith. Rom. 1:17. Gal. 3:11. Heb. 10:38. This is so because we accepted Jesus Christ as our Savior and Lord by faith. Eph. 3:17. Since this is the basis upon which we began this journey, it must be the basis for continuity and completion.

What is faith? Heb. 11:1 defines faith as the substance of things hoped for, the evidence of things not seen. Faith is substance and evidence. It is what you have until you hold it literally. The substance and evidence is God's word. That is the only thing that is real because it is God and God is Spirit. Spirits are more real than material things.

How do you know spirit? By words. Jesus said that the words I speak are spirits and they give life. John 6:63. When I hear God speak to me or I read Him in His word that is substance and evidence. I take His word and speak it. As I speak His word, I am releasing the spirit of that word to take dominion and domicile of that space. Eventually, the person or place I spoke those words take the size and shape of the spirit.

Water will always take the shape and size of the container. My body, bank account and business will take on the spirit I speak over them consistently. Keep saying that you are sick and tired, you will be. Keep saying that you are poor and broke, you will be. You take the size and shape of the spirits you speak over your life. I choose to speak differently because I know what I want to see.

As we continue making our confessions for the rest of the month, I want to remind you of what God said in Numbers 11:18-23. God promised to give you food the whole of this month.

<h2 style="text-align:center">CONFESSION FOR THE MONTH</h2>

I believe and declare,

The Lord is my Rock. He is large and solid for me. He can hold me just as I can hold Him. I choose to hold on to Him and His word in the name of Jesus Christ my Lord.

The Lord is my Fortress. He is my stronghold and defense headquarters. As long as I am in Him, no plague can penetrate me. I am safe in Him.

The Lord is my Deliverer. He causes me to escape every assault and attack from the enemy. I am delivered from the plague in the name of Jesus Christ my Lord.

The Lord is my God. I have no other God but Jehovah God. Jehovah Jireh is my God. The El Shaddai is my God. The government is not my God. My God is Supreme and Superior to all. His judgment nullifies all others.

The Lord is my Strength. He empowers, energizes and emboldens me to overcome all tests, trials, troubles, tribulations and temptations. I totally depend on the Lord who strengthens me to overcome this month in the name of Jesus Christ my Lord.

The Lord is my Buckler. He shields me from every dart, arrow and plague shot at me. He wards them off from me. That is why no plague touches me. No sickness or disease or infection or virus touches me. I am safe in Christ Jesus my Lord.

The Lord is the Horn of my Salvation. He saves me and keeps me safe. I am saved and safe in Christ Jesus my Lord.

The Lord is my High Tower. I am impervious and inaccessible to all plagues and pestilence. No evil shall befall me. No plague shall come near me. I have a vantage position. I am not disadvantaged. I have the advantage because the Lord is my High Tower.

The Lord is my Trust. I am secured, insured and assured because I trust in the Lord Jesus Christ. I am not moved by the government or economy or news. I am moved

by God's word that guarantees my security and supplies in the name of Jesus Christ my Lord. Amen.

As you make these confessions, watch out for what God is doing. He said that you will SEE His word works. See only His word. Nothing else.

DAY TWENTY-SIX

Welcome to the twenty sixth day of our confession of faith!

Do you want to know why Satan fights you to stop you from making your daily confessions of God's word? He knows the power of confession. It worked for him when he was Lucifer in heaven. He was beautiful because he worshipped God with words in songs. Words in song can make anyone beautiful. He saw how speaking well of God radiated shekinah glory. Ezek. 28:11-17. He forgot that it was his confession or speaking well of God that made him beautiful. When you speak well of God, His glory radiates on you.

"How art thou fallen from heaven, O Lucifer, son of the morning! how art thou cut down to the ground, which didst weaken the nations!

For thou hast said in thine heart, <u>I will</u> ascend into heaven, <u>I will</u> exalt my throne above the stars of God: <u>I will</u> sit also upon the mount of the congregation, in the sides of the north:

<u>I will</u> *ascend above the heights of the clouds;* <u>I will</u> *be like the most High."*

Isa. 14:12-14.

Five times Lucifer said, *I will...* He kept on making his confession about how he would be, what he would do, etc. We don't know for how long he kept making his confession until one third of the angels believed him and rebelled with him. Rev. 12:4.

Two things I learned from the Lucifer experiment are: one, If you keep speaking God's word, angels will believe you and follow you until you see God's word as your reality. Two, one third of the angels that rebelled with Lucifer couldn't help him achieve his confession. It took Michael and the remaining two third angels to kick out Lucifer and his angels out of heaven. I must make my confessions two to three times a day to make it happen.

Since the minimum is two third, I choose to make my confessions twice a day minimum like Joshua 1:8 tells me to meditate or chew on the word day and night.

To meditate is the same thing as saying it to myself, my situation and to someone else. Say it until they believe you and follow you. I am ready to make my confessions so that angels will believe and follow me to make God's word my reality.

As we continue making our confessions for the rest of the month, I want to remind you of what God said in Numbers 11:18-23. God promised to give you food the whole of this month.

CONFESSION FOR THE MONTH

I believe and declare,

The Lord is my Rock. He is large and solid for me. He can hold me just as I can hold Him. I choose to hold on to Him and His word in the name of Jesus Christ my Lord.

The Lord is my Fortress. He is my stronghold and defense headquarters. As long as I am in Him, no plague can penetrate me. I am safe in Him.

The Lord is my Deliverer. He causes me to escape every assault and attack from the enemy. I am delivered from the plague in the name of Jesus Christ my Lord.

The Lord is my God. I have no other God but Jehovah God. Jehovah Jireh is my God. The El Shaddai is my God. The government is not my God. My God is Supreme and Superior to all. His judgment nullifies all others.

The Lord is my Strength. He empowers, energizes and emboldens me to overcome all tests, trials, troubles, tribulations and temptations. I totally depend on the Lord who strengthens me to overcome this month in the name of Jesus Christ my Lord.

The Lord is my Buckler. He shields me from every dart, arrow and plague shot at me. He wards them off from me. That is why no plague touches me. No sickness or disease or infection or virus touches me. I am safe in Christ Jesus my Lord.

The Lord is the Horn of my Salvation. He saves me and keeps me safe. I am saved and safe in Christ Jesus my Lord.

The Lord is my High Tower. I am impervious and inaccessible to all plagues and pestilence. No evil shall befall me. No plague shall come near me. I have a vantage position. I am not disadvantaged. I have the advantage because the Lord is my High Tower.

The Lord is my Trust. I am secured, insured and assured because I trust in the Lord Jesus Christ. I am not moved by the government or economy or news. I am moved by God's word that guarantees my security and supplies in the name of Jesus Christ my Lord. Amen.

As you make these confessions, watch out for what God is doing. He said that you will SEE His word works. See only His word. Nothing else.

DAY TWENTY-SEVEN

Welcome to the twenty seventh day of our confession of faith!

In my book, **Putting Your Angels To Work**, I told several stories of my personal experience with angels working for me. This is one rich benefits of being a believer in Christ. God specially assigns angelic beings to serve you. Psalm 34:7. 91:11. Heb. 1:14.

Unfortunately, not many Christians know they have angels assigned to them. That's why they don't even know how to put them to work. For your information, these angels are awesome and awful in performance and presence.

One sure way to put your angels to work is the confession of God's word. When you speak well of God, you energize your angels to work for you. Even though they don't take orders from you directly, God's word in your confession becomes their direct orders. Psalm 103:20 shows us that they listen to God's word in your voice. That word is what they work on to provide for you, protect and preserve you. This is one reason I make my confessions daily so I can energize my angels to work for me.

"You who are his angels, praise the Lord.

You are the mighty warriors who do what he says

and who obey his voice."

Ps 103:20. New Century Version

Now I am ready to put my angels to work with my confession.

As we continue making our confessions for the rest of the month, I want to remind you of what God said in Numbers 11:18-23. God promised to give you food the whole of this month.

CONFESSION FOR THE MONTH

I believe and declare,

The Lord is my Rock. He is large and solid for me. He can hold me just as I can hold Him. I choose to hold on to Him and His word in the name of Jesus Christ my Lord.

The Lord is my Fortress. He is my stronghold and defense headquarters. As long as I am in Him, no plague can penetrate me. I am safe in Him.

The Lord is my Deliverer. He causes me to escape every assault and attack from the enemy. I am delivered from the plague in the name of Jesus Christ my Lord.

The Lord is my God. I have no other God but Jehovah God. Jehovah Jireh is my God. The El Shaddai is my God. The government is not my God. My God is Supreme and Superior to all. His judgment nullifies all others.

The Lord is my Strength. He empowers, energizes and emboldens me to overcome all tests, trials, troubles, tribulations and temptations. I totally depend on the Lord who strengthens me to overcome this month in the name of Jesus Christ my Lord.

The Lord is my Buckler. He shields me from every dart, arrow and plague shot at me. He wards them off from me. That is why no plague touches me. No sickness or disease or infection or virus touches me. I am safe in Christ Jesus my Lord.

The Lord is the Horn of my Salvation. He saves me and keeps me safe. I am saved and safe in Christ Jesus my Lord.

The Lord is my High Tower. I am impervious and inaccessible to all plagues and pestilence. No evil shall befall me. No plague shall come near me. I have a vantage position. I am not disadvantaged. I have the advantage because the Lord is my High Tower.

The Lord is my Trust. I am secured, insured and assured because I trust in the Lord Jesus Christ. I am not moved by the government or economy or news. I am moved by God's word that guarantees my security and supplies in the name of Jesus Christ my Lord. Amen.

As you make these confessions, watch out for what God is doing. He said that you will SEE His word works. See only His word. Nothing else.

DAY TWENTY-EIGHT

Welcome to the twenty eighth day of our confession of faith!

Angels are real. They were created by God's spoken word. John 1:1-3. Col. 1:16. By the law of creation, everything created functions by the creator and exist to please the creator. All creation functions by this rule directly or indirectly. No angel functions independent from God. They move by God's spoken word.

When you speak or say God's word, they follow that word. Before you allow the Devil to mess up your mind thinking if you qualify or if the word you speak will work, let me show you what Rev. 19:11-16 says. You will see why the spoken word works.

"And I saw heaven opened, and behold a white horse; and he that sat upon him was called Faithful and True, and in righteousness he doth judge and make war.

His eyes were as a flame of fire, and on his head were many crowns; and he had a name written, that no man knew, but he himself.

And he was clothed with a vesture dipped in blood: and his name is called The Word of God.

And the armies which were in heaven followed him upon white horses, clothed in fine linen, white and clean.

And out of his mouth goeth a sharp sword, that with it he should smite the nations: and he shall rule them with a rod of iron: and he treadeth the winepress of the fierceness and wrath of Almighty God.

And he hath on his vesture and on his thigh a name written, KING OF KINGS, AND Lord OF Lords."

Rev 19:11-16.

It is called Faithful and True. Anything that doesn't resemble the word is a lie. Don't say it. The spoken word is consistent. It doesn't fail. The word will work for you because it has been clothed with blood, the blood of Jesus Christ. The name of Jesus is the Word of God. Every time you confess the word, you are declaring, in fact, painting His name on that person or place or property. That gives Him ownership rights. He can never lose what He owns. John 10:29.

The knocker is in Rev. 19:14. It says that the armies of heaven follows the Word of God. One angel can destroy a whole continent like the Chinese virus has done so far. You think about an Army of angels following God's word in your mouth. There is no demon in hell or earth that can withstand the angelic force at your disposal. These angels are just waiting for you to utter the word and they take it from there.

My job is the easy part. Just speak the word. The Roman Centurion knew this when he told Jesus, *speak the word only and my servant shall be healed.* Matt. 8:8. His job is the hard part. He specializes in the hard or impossible. Luke 18:27. Now that you know your part, focus on doing it. Forget what people say. Do your part. Speak the word only.

Now I am ready to speak the word only and I shall see it come to pass in Jesus name. Amen.

As we continue making our confessions for the rest of the month, I want to remind you of what God said in Numbers 11:18-23. God promised to give you food the whole of this month.

CONFESSION FOR THE MONTH

I believe and declare,

The Lord is my Rock. He is large and solid for me. He can hold me just as I can hold Him. I choose to hold on to Him and His word in the name of Jesus Christ my Lord.

The Lord is my Fortress. He is my stronghold and defense headquarters. As long as I am in Him, no plague can penetrate me. I am safe in Him.

The Lord is my Deliverer. He causes me to escape every assault and attack from the enemy. I am delivered from the plague in the name of Jesus Christ my Lord.

The Lord is my God. I have no other God but Jehovah God. Jehovah Jireh is my God. The El Shaddai is my God. The government is not my God. My God is Supreme and Superior to all. His judgment nullifies all others.

The Lord is my Strength. He empowers, energizes and emboldens me to overcome all tests, trials, troubles, tribulations and temptations. I totally depend on the Lord who strengthens me to overcome this month in the name of Jesus Christ my Lord.

The Lord is my Buckler. He shields me from every dart, arrow and plague shot at me. He wards them off from me. That is why no plague touches me. No sickness or disease or infection or virus touches me. I am safe in Christ Jesus my Lord.

The Lord is the Horn of my Salvation. He saves me and keeps me safe. I am saved and safe in Christ Jesus my Lord.

The Lord is my High Tower. I am impervious and inaccessible to all plagues and pestilence. No evil shall befall me. No plague shall come near me. I have a vantage position. I am not disadvantaged. I have the advantage because the Lord is my High Tower.

The Lord is my Trust. I am secured, insured and assured because I trust in the Lord Jesus Christ. I am not moved by the government or economy or news. I am moved by God's word that guarantees my security and supplies in the name of Jesus Christ my Lord. Amen.

As you make these confessions, watch out for what God is doing. He said that you will SEE His word works. See only His word. Nothing else.

DAY TWENTY-NINE

Welcome to the twenty ninth day of our confession of faith!

Is it possible that some bad things that happen to us as Christians happen because we don't engage our angels to work for us? Does that mean that there are troubles we can avoid if we put our angels to work?

Look at Jesus, when He was tempted, He had no angelic assistance. He had to use the word to overcome. Angels only ministered to Him after the temptation. Matt. 4:11. I definitely need angelic ministration after every temptation.

However, when He was arrested and His disciples were ready to fight, He asked them a question: ***Don't you think that I cannot now pray to My Father and He shall presently give Me more than twelve legions of angels?*** Matt. 26:53.

A legion is a division of 3,000 to 6,000 men, including a complement of cavalry, in the ancient Roman army. That alone is too much. If one angel can destroy a continent, twelve legions will be like killing a mosquito with a machine gun.

The point Jesus made here was that He had access to more than twelve legions of angels if He wanted to fight. Another point is that they were just a spoken word away. Just a word from His mouth and you will see these hordes of angels ready to do His bidden.

Now, Jesus has bequeathed to you and me the same access. He has given us the same privilege. Can you imagine the hosts of angels waiting for you to say the word and they will be all over the place ready to do what the word from your mouth says?

Jesus didn't use that lifeline because of redemption plan. Matt. 26:54. However, you can either use it or miss it. I choose to use every privilege given to me by God.

It is for this reason I make my confessions daily because I want to see angels work for me.

As we continue making our confessions for the rest of the month, I want to remind you of what God said in Numbers 11:18-23. God promised to give you food the whole of this month.

CONFESSION FOR THE MONTH

I believe and declare,

The Lord is my Rock. He is large and solid for me. He can hold me just as I can hold Him. I choose to hold on to Him and His word in the name of Jesus Christ my Lord.

The Lord is my Fortress. He is my stronghold and defense headquarters. As long as I am in Him, no plague can penetrate me. I am safe in Him.

The Lord is my Deliverer. He causes me to escape every assault and attack from the enemy. I am delivered from the plague in the name of Jesus Christ my Lord.

The Lord is my God. I have no other God but Jehovah God. Jehovah Jireh is my God. The El Shaddai is my God. The government is not my God. My God is Supreme and Superior to all. His judgment nullifies all others.

The Lord is my Strength. He empowers, energizes and emboldens me to overcome all tests, trials, troubles, tribulations and temptations. I totally depend on the Lord who strengthens me to overcome this month in the name of Jesus Christ my Lord.

The Lord is my Buckler. He shields me from every dart, arrow and plague shot at me. He wards them off from me. That is why no plague touches me. No sickness or disease or infection or virus touches me. I am safe in Christ Jesus my Lord.

The Lord is the Horn of my Salvation. He saves me and keeps me safe. I am saved and safe in Christ Jesus my Lord.

The Lord is my High Tower. I am impervious and inaccessible to all plagues and pestilence. No evil shall befall me. No plague shall come near me. I have a vantage position. I am not disadvantaged. I have the advantage because the Lord is my High Tower.

The Lord is my Trust. I am secured, insured and assured because I trust in the Lord Jesus Christ. I am not moved by the government or economy or news. I am moved by God's word that guarantees my security and supplies in the name of Jesus Christ my Lord. Amen.

As you make these confessions, watch out for what God is doing. He said that you will SEE His word works. See only His word. Nothing else.

DAY THIRTY

Welcome to the thirtieth day of our confession of faith!

Today is the last day of this journey we began since the first day of this month.

> ***"Take my yoke upon you, and learn of me; for I am meek and lowly in heart: and ye shall find rest unto your souls.***
>
> ***For my yoke is easy, and my burden is light."***

Matt. 11:29-30.

One reason I love being a Christian is the fact that it is easy. Jesus said so. It is religion that makes it look hard. To become a Christian, you don't have to do or give anything especially for those who can't and don't have. All you have to do is to believe and confess. Rom. 10:8-13. What is so difficult about believing? It is a simple decision you make for yourself which no one can make for you. What is so difficult about confessing what you believe about Christ? It is so easy and simple. As easy and simple as that is, it totally transforms a sinner to a saint. That is the power of confession.

To continue living as a Christian is so easy too. It is as easy as making your daily confessions. Your life follows your words. Keep saying it and you will see it as your reality.

In order that you will never have any excuse for not living the Christian life as God planned for you, God gave us this tool of confession. What should you confess daily? Jesus! If you confess Him before men, He will confess you before His Father. You can't miss heaven when He is confessing you before the Father daily. Matt. 10:32. Even angels recognize you because He confesses you to them when you confess Him before men. Luke 12:8.

Just in case you are overwhelmed with your sins and shortcomings, all you need to do is to confess them to Him. No matter your sin, confess and forsake them and you are free. Prov. 28:13. I will never allow my sin to deprive me of a beautiful relationship with God and that is why I confess them to Him and forsake them. 1 John 1:9.

Even if I sin, why people are judging me, I know who forgives me. I run to Him and His job is to forgive me. 1 John 2:1-2. Always remember that His name Jesus simply means He saves those who sin. All I have to do to enjoy the rich benefits of His saving power is to call on Him. Acts 2:21. 2 Sam. 22:4. Joel 2:32. It is so simple that you don't have any excuse anymore.

Are your faults overwhelming you? By the way, everyone has a fault. There is no human being without one. So don't beat yourself up. You have done enough to yourself. Now use His prescribed cure for your faults. James 5:16-18. Confess your faults and pray. Pray from your heart and watch what God does with people like you. If He could use Elijah, He can use you with all your faults.

You can never have another day with depression or disappointment or discouragement because your confession can reroute your journey, redirect your energy and rewrite your story.

As we make our confessions for the last day of this month, I want to remind you of what God said in Numbers 11:18-23. God promised to give you food the whole of this month. I would love to read your testimony of how He fed you this whole month because I am a witness to this word. He has kept His word to me and my family. Please, share your testimony with me.

CONFESSION FOR THE MONTH

I believe and declare,

The Lord is my Rock. He is large and solid for me. He can hold me just as I can hold Him. I choose to hold on to Him and His word in the name of Jesus Christ my Lord.

The Lord is my Fortress. He is my stronghold and defense headquarters. As long as I am in Him, no plague can penetrate me. I am safe in Him.

The Lord is my Deliverer. He causes me to escape every assault and attack from the enemy. I am delivered from the plague in the name of Jesus Christ my Lord.

The Lord is my God. I have no other God but Jehovah God. Jehovah Jireh is my God. The El Shaddai is my God. The government is not my God. My God is Supreme and Superior to all. His judgment nullifies all others.

The Lord is my Strength. He empowers, energizes and emboldens me to overcome all tests, trials, troubles, tribulations and temptations. I totally depend on the Lord who strengthens me to overcome this month in the name of Jesus Christ my Lord.

The Lord is my Buckler. He shields me from every dart, arrow and plague shot at me. He wards them off from me. That is why no plague touches me. No sickness or disease or infection or virus touches me. I am safe in Christ Jesus my Lord.

The Lord is the Horn of my Salvation. He saves me and keeps me safe. I am saved and safe in Christ Jesus my Lord.

The Lord is my High Tower. I am impervious and inaccessible to all plagues and pestilence. No evil shall befall me. No plague shall come near me. I have a vantage position. I am not disadvantaged. I have the advantage because the Lord is my High Tower.

The Lord is my Trust. I am secured, insured and assured because I trust in the Lord Jesus Christ. I am not moved by the government or economy or news. I am moved by God's word that guarantees my security and supplies in the name of Jesus Christ my Lord. Amen.

As you make these confessions, watch out for what God is doing. He said that you will SEE His word works. See only His word. Nothing else.

OFFERING TIME

Give your offering to spite the plague. Plant your seed to GTBank account number 0038894924. From anywhere in the world, you can use MoneyGram to send your offering to the account number for free.

In Nigeria, you can give your offering by using your bank code as follows:

For offering, dial: *bankcode*000*491+amount#

For tithes, dial: *bankcode*000*492+amount#

If you are using GTBank for instance, your bank code is 737. So you can dial, *737*000*491+amount#

If you are in the United States of America, you can give your offering to Bank of America account number 000905418443. ABA routing number 121000358.

If you are in the United Kingdom, you can give your offering to NatWest account 52344819. Sort code 602112.

YOUR FEEDBACK

One of my best songs is **Excess Love** by Mercy Chinwo. It is actually my song that God gave her to sing for me. I sing and play that song like a hundred times a day. That song has been viewed by ten million viewers on YouTube. It has forty thousand likes and three thousand four hundred dislikes.

If you have ever listened to that song, like me, you will enjoy it even if it is the only song on earth. It is a fine song. It fits my kind of life. Yet, there are over three thousand people who don't like it.

Life lesson: even at your very best with all your packaging, you will still have several thousands who will never like you.

What is my point? Assuming like that song, you were designed by God to reach at least ten million people. Out of them, only forty thousand likes you and three thousand four hundred dislikes, despises and disdains you. My question is, will you focus your energy on the dislikes or the likes or those you are wired for?

Jesus knew people so He, *"...didn't entrust His life to them. He knew them inside and out, knew how untrustworthy they were. He didn't need any help in seeing right through them."* John 2:23-25. Message Version.

Throughout the month, I started sharing with you daily devotions to help you through the month in obedience to God's word. He promised to feed us in spite of the lockdown. I have seen God's provision this past month of April, 2020. I will be glad to read your testimony of God's provision for you and your family.

Will you be kind to send me your testimony? I just want to know out of the ten million, the forty thousand who have been blessed by these devotionals. If you are among those who were upset, please, don't bother to respond.

Thank you very much for your kind feedback.

WHY I CHOSE JESUS CHRIST?

Someone asked me many years ago, Mike, why did you accept Jesus Christ? I could have become an atheist, a Muslim, etc. Why Jesus Christ?

My answer to that question is for basically three reasons and the fourth one will blow your mind.

One, I accepted Jesus Christ because I needed a Father. A father is a life source. That means you came from him. According to the law of sustenance, you can only be sustained by your source. Fish came out of water and thus can only be sustained in a water environment. If you put it on land, no matter how nice looking, it will die in no distant time. I realized that God is my Source. I can only be sustained by Him. I discovered that I couldn't have a personal relationship with Him through any other one or way except through Jesus Christ. John 14:6. Acts 4:12.

Like a fish out of water in a land environment, you and I continue to struggle to survive until we reconnect with our natural habitat or source. This is God your Father. This happens only through Jesus Christ. You will never be fulfilled or become eternally relevant until you accept Jesus Christ into your heart as your personal Lord and Master. Then will you be able to connect with God your Source. Then will you know what it means to be sustained by the grace of God.

Two, I accepted Jesus Christ because I needed a friend. Man was designed to relate with his environment and people. Nobody can survive as an island. You will need friends in your life. For me, it is very easy to make friends. As I grew up, my life became messed up by the friends I had. Friends betrayed me. Some battered me. Yet some others left me each time after our relationship with bruises. The marks will always be there. It was my search unknown to me for the real friend that got me into such relationships. I did not know about the Friend that sticks closer than a brother. Proverbs 18:24.

Friends have scorned me like they did Job. Job's friends turned aside from him (Job 6:18). They laughed him to scorn (Job 12:4). He was such a laughing stock that his eyes poured out tears to God (Job 16:20). His kinfolks failed him. His friends forgot him (Job 19:14). I have been there.

I needed a friend who will love me the way I am. I found this Friend in Jesus. He is God who became Abraham's Friend (Gen. 18:17. 2 Chron. 20:7). What a Friend He was to Abraham that even when Abraham lied about his wife, God rebuked the king to restore Abraham's wife (Gen. 12:10-20. 20:1-18.). A true friend will be there for you in good times and bad ones. Jesus is the best Friend I have ever had in my life. (John 15:14).

You will never know a true friend outside of Jesus Christ. Your parents? Spouse? Relatives? Classmates? Colleagues? I chose Jesus Christ because He will be there for me all the time. He said so and I believe Him.

Three, I needed a future. Life is past, present and future. I have seen the past; it was both good and bad. I cannot do anything about it. It is gone forever. I failed in the past. I did all the bad things in the past. But it is gone leaving me with the consequences of my wrong choices and deeds. Now I am in the present. What can I do to make the difference for my future? This is what I am concerned with today. I discovered that it is only in Jesus Christ that His precious blood washes my past away. My today is secured with His ever-abiding presence because He is a very present help. My tomorrow is taken care of because He told me not to worry about it.

I have a beautiful future in Jesus Christ because of what He did for me at the cross. I sinned and deserved to die. He took my sins and died in my place. In exchange, He gave me His very life, abundant life.

The fourth reason is that He changed my life. Religion tries to change people by principles, philosophies and practices. But Jesus came into my life without Him putting any demands on me to do things to earn His forgiveness. All He asked from me was to believe and receive Him. I did and found that my life is just changing every day. When I started this journey, I did not look like what I am today. I am not the same every day. I can assure you that by tomorrow I will become better. Until the day when I shall be changed permanently at the sound of the trump of God. From that point, I will put on immortality and incorruption. Sin shall never have dominion over me for all eternity. Is this not the kind of life you really desire from the deepest part of your being?

Today, my friend, you must make up your mind to receive Jesus Christ or reject Him. It is your choice. If you want to choose Jesus Christ, it is easy. Just say out loud:

Jesus, I believe You came to this world because You love me. Your love constrained You to the cross where You died for my sins. Jesus, I believe. Come into my heart today. Wash me with Your precious blood. Make me a new person whose love and passion will be for You the rest of my life on earth. Jesus, You are the Lord of my life from this day forward. Thank You for saving me in Jesus name. Amen.

If you have prayed this prayer, do write me today and I will send you some materials to help you in this journey to become all that God has designed you to be.

FOR MORE INFORMATION

You can enjoy the anointed ministry of the author through the many books he has written, his powerful messages on audiotapes, video and compact dics. Also by radio, television and internet. Use the address available below.

If God has blessed you through this ministry, send in your testimony today. We like to read or hear from you what God has done through this ministry. Someone can be saved, healed, helped and lifted up by your testimony.

Send in your prayer requests as well. Our God answers prayers today and always.

Take a bold step to partner with us as we strive to fulfill the God given mandate to reach thirty million souls in at least fifty countries of the world within the shortest possible time and through every available means. You can make online donations through our secure and safe web site. You can use your credit or debit cards at any time.

You can also purchase our products online. Just log on today

For more spiritual help, counseling and prayer ministration, contact:

Bishop Michael O. Amamieye

Michael Amamieye Word Outreach International

a/k/a Aggressive Faith Ministries

Plot 13 Walter Akpana Lay Out

Off 394 Ikwerre Road Mile 5 Rumueprikom

P. O. Box 12378

Port Harcourt, Nigeria.

Phone: +234-901800MAWO, 08050987377 (Nigeria)

+1-916-245-6157 (U.S.A.)

E-mail: info@aggressivefaith.org

Web site: www.aggressivefaith.org